Our Familiars

Anne Coombs

Anne Coombs was a journalist, author, political activist, and philanthropist. She authored five books, including *No Man's Land* (Simon & Schuster, 1993), *Sex and Anarchy: The life and death of the Sydney Push* (Viking, 1996) and *Broometime* (Hodder Headline, 2001), co-authored with Susan Varga. Her final novel, *Glass Houses*, was published in 2023 by Upswell.

Anne was one of the founders of Rural Australians for Refugees. She was a board member and chair of GetUp! She shared a passion with her partner for a fairer Australia, advocating for refugees and people seeking asylum.

In recent years Anne was a frequent essayist and commentator, and a regular contributor to the Griffith Review. She also wrote a feature film script set in Australia's far north, currently being developed for production.

Anne died at her Exeter home in December 2021.

Anne Coombs

Our Familiars

The meaning of animals in our lives

First published in Australia in 2024
by Upswell Publishing
Perth, Western Australia
upswellpublishing.com

Upswell operates in the city of Perth, on ancient country of the Whadjuk people of the Noongar nation who remain the spiritual and cultural custodians of this beautiful land. We acknowledge their continuing connection to country and express gratitude to elders past and present for their strength and creativity…Always was, always will be, Aboriginal land.

This book is copyright. Apart from any fair dealing for the purpose of private study, research, criticism or review, as permitted under the *Copyright Act 1968*, no part may be reproduced by any process without written permission. Enquiries should be made to the publisher.

Copyright © 2024 The estate of Anne Coombs

The moral right of the author has been asserted.

ISBN: 978-0-645-87459-4

A catalogue record for this book is available from the National Library of Australia

Cover design by Chil3, Fremantle
Typeset in Foundry Origin by Lasertype
Printed by McPherson's Printing Group

There is an unbreakable connection between
the observer and the observed.
John Barrow, *The World Within the World*

Contents

Preface: Elsie   9

PART ONE

    Chapter 1: Our Twenty Acres   15

    Chapter 2: The Forbidden Word   22

    Chapter 3: Through a New Lens   33

    Chapter 4: Farm Animals and Ethics   39

    Chapter 5: Animals in the Dock   44

    Chapter 6: The Company of Cats   51

    Chapter 7: Friendships Across Species   58

    Chapter 8: Familiarity and Difference   66

    Chapter 9: Why Scientists tie Themselves into Linguistic Knots   73

    Chapter 10: Communication   80

    Chapter 11: Do Animals Have Souls?   90

    Chapter 12: Animal Rights—and Wrongs   98

    Chapter 13: The Implications of Consciousness   105

PART TWO

    Chapter 14: Bird Brains   115

    Chapter 15: What Is 'Natural' to Animals?   122

Chapter 16: Observing Other Species 132

Chapter 17: Cross-species Empathy and Cooperation 139

Chapter 18: No Expectations 150

Chapter 19: The Healing Power of Animals 158

Chapter 20: Life and Death 164

Chapter 21: A New Farm, a Different Life 170

PART THREE

Chapter 22: Some Time Has Passed 181

Chapter 23: Complications 189

Chapter 24: A Very Hard Decision 193

Chapter 25: A Last Move 197

Chapter 26: In Times of Crisis 204

Afterword by Susan Varga 211

An Update: The Cast of Animals (and Two Humans) 219

Notes 221

Select Bibliography 225

Preface
Elsie

She had a little triangular tuft of tail that stuck up in the air and quivered frantically whenever a human approached, and protruding eyes of a beseeching light brown. Whenever she saw you she would stand on her back legs in excitement and bleat imploringly. She tried to speak but as a goat her repertoire was limited. Or maybe I didn't really listen, because the timbre of her call said it all, really: Where are you? Why have you left me here? Why am I alone? Why can't I belong?

Her name was Elsie and her job was to eat lantana and blackberry, and other weeds that managed to survive among those woody stems. She was tethered and the chain was always entangled, her water bucket always knocked over. Untangling her, filling her bucket, moving the tether occasionally; these were the extent of our ministrations. She was like an outcast kept beyond the village, provided with the barest essentials for survival but disparaged and ignored. I was a child and I was fond of her but didn't allow myself to be drawn into her distress.

Her white coat was often dirty, gritty because she lived among dirt and weeds. The bones of her legs were so fine you could encircle them with your fingers. She danced around us as we tended her. Yes, we were all fond of her. You couldn't not be fond of Elsie.

Elsie. I don't know where she came from, or where she went to after her 'job' with us was done. I don't remember when she ceased to be around. And after forty years I am suddenly fearful of what her life might have become. Could it have got worse? Oh yes. Far worse.

We were not cruel to her, beyond the common cruelty of containment, discomfort, loneliness and loss of freedom. Perhaps it was through Elsie that I learnt to harden my heart in the way of all those who have ever husbanded animals. To care for them and not really care for them. Ah, that was the trick!

Elsie's plaintive cries, her quivering tail and the clear and direct expression in her eyes all sought to open a channel between us, one that had to be resisted, or so it seemed to me then. Because where would it end? What she was asking for seemed bottomless. Nothing less than love. I believe she would have moved into my bedroom with me and lived there quite happily, revelling in the company. Such was the level of her loneliness.

But at eleven I was a good little husbander in the making. And she was a goat with a job to do. So I left her among the lantana stalks, rain, hail or shine. When it was very hot my father made sure she was tethered somewhere where there was some shade, and when it had been wet I often took an old sack down and gave her a bit of a rub dry.

Years later, when I bought my first piece of land, where I could have a few animals, I decided to get a pair of goats. Two, so they always had company. And I built them a stoutly fenced paddock so they never had to be tethered. And they had a shed where they could shelter from the weather. I often sat with them and talked with them. Their names were Jo and Flo. But not once—not when I acquired them, not when I built their paddock and shelter—did I think of Elsie. Yet now it is clear to me that Elsie's life was the palimpsest beneath their own.

I was making amends, creating a story I could be proud of.

*

Open any newspaper on almost any day and there will be stories of animals and their relationship with humans: inner-city parks crowded with dog-owners and their canine companions; orang-utans dying because of human destruction of their habitat; dolphins cavorting among swimmers at a popular beach. We share our world with these other creatures—they are part of our reality, as we are part of theirs. But have we lived with them in ignorance of their true natures? Have we been wilfully prejudiced? We discount animals and their abilities, even as we celebrate the occasional 'special' animal that proves itself almost our equal—and, in appearing different from others of its kind, merely reinforces *our* uniqueness.

Our lives cross with those of so many other people in the course of a life. But what of all the animals our lives intersect with? I can't even recall all the domestic animals—the dogs, cats, horses—that have been part of my life. It is almost profligate, this gathering of lives around you, only to disperse them or watch them die. And it's not necessary. People live without animals. Even I have managed to live without animals for brief periods. Yet, for some of us, a society made up only of our own kind feels colourless. The variety of other species, their strangeness and comedy, the tantalising glimpses of commonality sometimes seen in a face or a movement, are an essential reminder of our place in the world – in both the way we have dominated and how so much that goes on in the natural world is hidden from us.

While we have been fascinated by fictional speculations about alien life forms elsewhere in the universe, all the while, all around us on this earth, alien societies have been going about their business right in front of us. David Attenborough has opened the eyes of many of us to this. The insects and spiders and nocturnal creatures, the ants and bees, the birds and fishes. But while their habits have been documented, it is still a stretch to suggest that they might have lives as meaningful as ours. And what of the domestic animals that we surround ourselves with, and the farm animals in the paddock—how well do we know them?

It is sobering to think of all these creatures as our companions on the globe. We dominate them, but they survive—those that do survive. Perhaps there's no need to imagine alien universes. All we need do is open our minds, use our much-vaunted creative imaginations, and really see them, perhaps for the first time.

PART ONE

Chapter 1
Our Twenty Acres

We have lived here on our twenty acres for eighteen years. I know its hills and deep gullies like my own skin. When Susan and I found Keil-na-nain we were looking for a quiet and beautiful place where we could both write. But we weren't sure if this move to the country would work for us. We said we would try it for two years. The two years came and went.

Even after all these years I am still largely ignorant of the native plants and animals. Eucalypts, yes, but what sorts? Wallabies, yes, but what sorts? Years before we came here the farm was declared a wildlife refuge but I only recently received the first ever communication from the government about it, asking if we'd like a permanent conservation agreement. They wanted to know what habitats we have. What kind of vegetation? What native animals, rare or otherwise? I could give only the most general observations and make lame notes about our attempts to get rid of blackberries.

How assiduously we study our garden, know the flowers and shrubs, the creepers and bulbs. A cool climate garden—it was one of the things that drew Susan and me to the Highlands. And the European trees! Yet over the fence: almost nothing. Is it a lack of curiosity or simply the always-thereness of the bush? I walk the tracks each day: I know where certain weeds grow, where the clover is thick and lush, where native grasses and weeds predominate. Or where the groundcover is sparse, the clay soil showing through. But that's it. I've taken it for granted. Familiarity has dulled both sight and senses. And perhaps something similar has happened with my attitude to domestic animals.

I've spent my entire life around animals, and mostly been caring but unsentimental about them. I've always talked to them: not just the cats and dogs but the horses, cows and chooks. I talk to them in a companionable way, letting them become accustomed to the sound of my voice, in the belief that it makes them more tractable and cooperative. I've done it almost automatically most of the time, not thinking much about it. In fact, that has been my way with animals in general: not thinking much about them.

But having animals in one's life, being responsible for another living creature, is awe-inspiring if we allow ourselves to feel it. And now I am trying to live with them in a new way: to really watch. What things might they teach me, not only about themselves but about me? I'm aware of layers of being that I've barely registered.

*

We have recently become custodians of a new cat, Charlie. He is our first new 'house' animal for many years. Before Charlie arrived we were reduced to one very old dog, Jackie, who we have believed to be on her last legs for the past six years. The other cats and dogs had slowly died off and been ceremoniously buried in the orchard or—in the case of two dogs—cremated and their ashes kept on the mantelpiece.

Charlie came from the animal shelter, a kind of limbo land that hovers between heaven and hell. In the case of the local one, that is almost literally true. The council provided a small patch of land beside the rubbish dump for the shelter. The stench of the tip hovers over the collection of demountables that house the animals. Once inside, the stench fades: there is air-conditioning and loving staff, plentiful food and warm blankets. Charlie was in a cage by himself: about eighteen months old, grey and chubby-cheeked and with big yellow eyes. I'd already seen a few nice cats but none had drawn me as Charlie did. I picked him up out of his cage and he put his paws on my shoulders, leant into my neck and immediately began purring loudly. He was still a tom, and had a tear in one ear to attest that he'd seen a scrap or two. But he was clearly ready to be loved.

Charlie is only my third cat in the last thirty years and each one has played a major part in my life, companions on different stages of the journey. Constants, often not thought about too much, but always *there*. A permanent source of enjoyment, laughter and company. They make me smile. Between each cat, I spent a catless year. It wasn't an intentional period of mourning but it did seem to take me that long to be ready for another cat.

Charlie has quite a few dog-like characteristics. He likes being taken for walks, and he comes when called by his name. Sometimes he even does what he is told.

When one has always lived with animals, trying to live with them in a new way is hard; sometimes it feels almost impossible. Trying to live with them in a way that is not sentimental yet gives full acknowledgement of their sentience means constantly watching oneself, catching oneself on the cusp of brusqueness or indifference. Or, conversely, on the verge of mawkishness. They are so aware of what goes on around them, so sensitive. And, usually, in the case of domesticated animals at least, so powerless to change the circumstances of their lives.

*

When my father was dying and in the hospice, there was a big black and white cat that liked to lie on his bed. Dad was past saying much—he hadn't said much for years, come to think of it—but he clearly enjoyed having the cat nearby. A softness came over his face. Seeing that, I realised with a pang that he had always been fond of cats and in recent years one of his first questions when I spoke with him was always 'How's that cat of yours?' He loved animals and had been surrounded by them when we were growing up. In old age, he and my mother lived without pets. I wonder now if that wasn't such a great idea. He never said he wanted a pet—he wouldn't. He'd always pretended unsentimentality around animals and yet really he was a big softy.

Like a lot of country men (he was one by inclination rather than birth), he talked tough when it came to animals but often acted soft. I remember in particular the young black and white calf, Lily, that he hand-raised in the shed when she looked like dying. He refused to let her die. I'm unsure now what was wrong with her. Had she been bitten by something, or been half sucked dry by ticks? There were a lot of ticks about. She lay on a bed of sacking in the shed that doubled as a feed room, and later was suspended in a special sling he made for her, and he nursed her with bottled milk—getting up two or three times during the night. She lived, of course, and would later follow him around like a dog, or as if he were her parent.

Now that I am thinking back on the animals I have known I am surprised how often my father is there at the edge of the scene. It's not surprising really. I was not a child to be inside making dolls dresses or learning to bake biscuits. I was always out in the yard or paddock and so was he. Even now Susan tells me that I am always disappearing just as we are about to go out; always off moving a horse or shutting a gate. Like Dad.

*

Why is it, I wonder, that animals have been such a large part of my life? And why is that the case with so many people? And, given that, why is it that we have paid so little attention to them, I mean real attention, as in taking them seriously as subjects of their own lives?

They give us something, perhaps, that other parts of our life cannot: unconditional love, or so we like to think; a godlike sense of importance in the eyes of another living creature. Indeed, physical connection with a living thing is perhaps more important than ever now that so many of us spend our daily lives in cyberspace. They give us access to a more primitive, less censoring, more intuitive part of ourselves. My animals have been my companions through dark days. I suspect I am not alone in revealing my true self to them much more readily than I do to people. Animals allow us to express what we won't show another person.

I'm reminded of George, our old tough-minded philosopher friend, whom we drove down to the country one weekend on the same day that we collected a new kitten. All the way from the city to the farm George sat in the back seat crooning to the kitten: 'What a gorgeous little Sammy you are. Yes little Sammy, special little Sammy. Come to George', etc., etc. Susan and I sat in the front of the car, rolling our eyes at each other. Never had we heard such endearments from George.

Another source of fascination is that we can speculate on what an animal might be feeling but can we ever really *know*? The animal communicators will say we can but for most of us, the true thoughts and feelings of animals are always out of reach. They are so familiar to us—the cat on the doorstep, the dog at the gate—but unknowable. We can feel that we understand our animals, and know what they are thinking, but that is *our* feeling, not theirs.

They are the ultimate mystery, maybe in part because they are so commonplace, so *there*, so part of our everyday lives.

Every evening when my horse Vincent comes in from the paddock, he stands at his stable window, all his attention fixed on the glorious view down the valley. He ignores me, eyes only on whatever it is that so fascinates him as the light begins to fade. He does this every evening. What is so fascinating? Will I ever know?

The cows in the paddock, the chooks in their pen, the bull surrounded by his little team of baby steers. Each has a life with a shape to it and a meaning, and I believe each has a sense of being alive. We live side by side in overlapping bubbles. They are my familiars, more familiar, if I am honest, than most of my friends. They are part of the rhythm of my days, like a musical accompaniment to my thinking self. I can't go so far as to say I have individual relationships with the cattle or the hens, nor do I need to. Each has a purpose and abilities that invest their life with meaning. If they are prevented from living out their purpose they, too, can become frustrated, bored or neurotic, much as we do. They are on their life's path and I am on mine, and they run in parallel.

It seems it is a little different with the cats and dogs and horses, the ones we are inclined to consider 'family', the ones we love. Of all the animals we have at present, it is the donkey, Lina, with whom I feel most able to communicate, who I feel most truly understands what I am saying to her. When she is in pain I empathise and it comforts her; and when I am in pain she empathises and it comforts me. It doesn't matter if the pain is physical or mental, both are of equal significance to her, of that I am sure.

But how do I know this? I know it by the tilt of her ears and the expression in her eyes when I talk to her, by the way she snuffles my hair with her muzzle when she comforts me, by the way she leans her head against me when I comfort her, by the way she stands so patiently when I am tending her sore foot, by the way she calls out in frustration when she is lonely or unhappy. By her quiet contentment when we are together. By my utter trust in her and the way she will allow me to do almost anything with her, which shows her trust in me.

How can we ascertain what they are feeling or thinking, and can we?

What are we to them?

What are the factional divides among animal lovers, and why? What are the theoretical differences?

How have ideas about animals and animal behaviours and animal emotions changed over time? And what will be the result if we take the growing respect for animal rights and animals' feelings to their logical conclusion?

These are all the themes I want to explore.

But first, a word about my title, *Our Familiars*. The word 'familiars' is not much in common use, but I have chosen it because of its multiple levels of meaning, rooted in the word 'family'.

In the first sense, it is about the way animals *become* family, as we live with them so closely, observe them daily, and come to love them deeply.

In the second, related, sense they are 'familiar' to us because of their very proximity—their habits, their routines. They are part of everyday life. We feed, walk, ride, groom them, watch TV with them, and put them to bed. Sometimes *in* our bed…

They are familiar as old shoes. We hardly notice that we relate to them across species and without language. I'm talking of dogs and cats, but also of horses, chooks, pets of every description, and some farm animals, too.

In the third, less known, sense, familiars are associated with supernatural beliefs. In medieval folklore, familiars were believed to be supernatural beings who could assist witches in their magic and often assumed the form of an animal.

Historian Emma Wilby, who specialises in early modern magical beliefs, describes how familiars have traditionally come to the aid of humans as they struggled to survive an enduring lack of food or money, sickness and bereavement.

In all the senses I've mentioned, the term 'familiars' opens up even more avenues of thought. What do animals mean to us? And what do we mean to them?

Chapter 2
The Forbidden Word

Some years after he wrote *The Origin of Species*, Charles Darwin published another book that could in some ways be seen as a continuation of that earlier work. *The Expression of the Emotions in Man and Animals* started from the assumption that all of us, all of us animals, have a common background and so are bound to have characteristics in common. Darwin was a well-established figure by this time and his work was read avidly. But there was still a real reluctance to accept his underlying thesis. For Darwin, there was nothing shocking in the idea that humans and other animals might share many characteristics. In endeavouring to link the expression of emotion in animals with similar displays in people, he was teasing out the characteristics which are learned from those that are instinctive. But he also saw an 'instinct' as something that came about for a reason; it, too, was 'learnt' at some point. So often the actions of animals are dismissed as merely instinctive, which begs the question, 'how did that instinct develop?'

Scientists speak of the 'flight response', the 'nurturing instinct' and even 'pleasure response', rather than use words like fear, love and enjoyment. The language of common sense is abandoned because it is seen as anthropomorphic—a charge which for many years would have led to academic death. But surely at some point, some animal must have felt fear to learn a 'flight response'?

Darwin said, 'Actions, which were at first voluntary, soon became habitual, and at last hereditary, and may then be performed even in opposition to the will.'[1]

Darwin's writing was charmingly matter-of-fact. 'We may confidently believe that laughter, as a sign of pleasure or enjoyment, was practised by our progenitors long before they deserved to be called human; for very many kinds of monkeys, when pleased, utter a reiterated sound, clearly analogous to our laughter, often accompanied by vibratory movements of their jaws or lips, with the corners of the mouth drawn backwards and upwards, by the wrinkling of the cheeks, and even by the brightening of the eyes.'[2]

For him it was a matter of great interest, not blasphemy, to ponder the chain of connection between humans and other animals. He called non-human animals 'lower animals' because this terminology fitted not only his theory of evolution but also contemporary attitudes. He gathered material, too, on the expression of emotion in 'primitive' people—part of the chain, lower humans. Darwin was of his time, even if he was a radical.

'The movements of expression in the face and body, whatever their origin may have been, are in themselves of much importance for our welfare. They serve as the first means of communication between the mother and her infant; she smiles approval, and thus encourages her child on the right path, or frowns disapproval. We readily perceive sympathy in others by their expression; our sufferings are thus mitigated and our pleasures increased; and mutual good feeling is thus strengthened. The movements of expression give vividness and energy to our spoken words. They reveal the thoughts and intentions of others more truly than do words, which may be falsified.'[3]

There has been a deep reluctance by people to accept that we are not some singular and divine creation. Darwin was in part writing in response to Charles Bell's 1806 *Essays on Anatomy and Physiology of Expression in Painting*. Bell, a Scottish surgeon, anatomist and artist—best known today for describing the facial paralysis Bell's palsy—believed that human facial muscles were divinely created to express our unique and exquisite feelings. Bell concluded that such expressions were found only in humans.[4] But if I smile at my dog he knows I am pleased, and if I frown at him he sinks, with his tail between his legs, chastised.

The weight of thought from Aristotle to Descartes has held that humans are at the top of the hierarchy and that animals are here to serve man's interests. Nineteenth-century scientific rationalism, built on a foundation of Christian prejudice, has dominated thinking about the nature of animals. Yet, simultaneously, many writers have described the special talents and abilities of animals. The attitude of one anonymous nineteenth-century writer is typical: '[Man's] is a delegated right from the great Author of his being; to him was assigned the dominion of every living thing that moveth upon the earth.'[5] Yet this same author wrote beautifully of the true nature of dogs:

'Without being endowed like man with reason, his feelings, if the expression may be allowed, are extremely delicate, and he has, generally speaking, greater fidelity and steadiness of affection. He is neither to be corrupted by ambition, interest, nor the desire for revenge; he is all zeal, ardour and obedience—more apt to recall benefits than outrages; he is not even discouraged by blows and hard usage, but calmly suffers, and soon forgets them...He is, perhaps, the only animal whose fidelity is unshaken.'[6]

The writer notes that the ubiquity of dogs around the world has prevented us from appreciating their true character: 'While almost every other quadruped fears man as its most formidable enemy, here is one that regards him as a companion, and follows him as a friend.'[7]

The anonymous author of *Domesticated Animals; Considered with reference to Civilization and the Arts* calls this a 'successful subjugation' of the dog but recent researchers now feel that the domestication of dogs may have been a two-way process, that it might perhaps even be that dogs domesticated man. Such a scenario makes a certain sense. Wild dogs, lurking on the edge of human habitation, may well have found it to their benefit to deepen the acquaintance—we are all familiar with the stray who hangs around hoping for a feed. Perhaps the original wild dogs found that they could live cooperatively with human beings: help with the hunt and they could get a portion of the prize. This mutually dependent relationship between human and dog has existed for many thousands of years. The earliest known evidence of dog domestication dates back to the late Stone Age, when a canine was buried in present-day Bonn, Germany, alongside a man and woman. The remains of all three, uncovered about a century ago, have been identified as more than 14,000 years old.[8] Cave drawings discovered south-east of Cairo in 2000 date back to 7000 BCE and clearly show men and women hunting with dogs by their sides. Australian Aborigines are thought to have hunted with dingoes from around 4000 BCE.

Dogs are said to be the only animal that relate more to members of another species—human beings—than to members of their own species. That is an extraordinary thing. So intertwined have we become that it is now believed that many dogs don't see humans as another species. If this is so, it is even more incumbent upon us to learn to speak dog.

*

In interacting with our own animals we often believe there is a real connection. It is now increasingly fashionable to pay attention to that connection, perhaps even to the extent of trying to recapture an intuitive ability to communicate with animals that early humans may have had and that we have lost. The shamans and witches who could 'talk to the animals' are the things of myth. But modern-day equivalents are emerging, people who believe that we can recover and develop this intuitive connection with other species.

This is the belief of American animal communicator Marta Williams. Williams comes from a scientific background and has been at pains to develop a series of exercises and experiments whereby students of animal communication can test their accuracy. The 'sixth sense' that many of us have, whereby we know who is on the phone before we pick it up, or feel uneasy about something having happened to someone we love—these are the remnants of our intuition and can be built on, according to Williams. Tuning into an animal, asking it questions, 'hearing' its response. Whacky as it sounds, something is fascinating about this idea. Who among us who has ever loved a cat or dog has not said to a friend or family member at some stage: 'I could swear she knew what I was saying'?

So I decided to give it a try. The three most likely candidates among my own menagerie seemed to be Charlie the cat, Lina the donkey and my horse Vincent. Charlie has been a very interactive cat from the day he arrived so talking to him came naturally. The fact that he came when called by name in an ordinary voice and seemed ready to 'listen' was an advantage. Simply focusing on him and spending more time with him seemed to make him readier to partake of conversation. Having Charlie around is like having a very well-behaved and self-sufficient house guest who keeps to themselves when you are busy, is happy to just sit in the sun, but is also ready for an intense and lively conversation whenever you feel so inclined.

After a week or two of such discussions Charles and I seemed to be on a very good footing together. What made me think there might be something in this conversation business was one Sunday afternoon when I decided to have a nap. Charlie wanted to come onto the bed with me. Fair enough, as long as he stayed in the bottom corner of the bed—his corner. As I began to try to sleep, Charlie was energetically cleaning himself, while purring loudly, making an unholy racket. I put up with it for five minutes, then said sternly: 'If you don't lie down and go to sleep right now, I will put you out.'

He immediately stopped purring, curled up in a ball, and went completely quiet. Both of us then had an hour's blissful sleep.

Lina has always enjoyed human company. Unlike a lot of donkeys, she is very easy to handle. She loves being groomed and having her long ears rubbed—slowly, gently, standing in front of her, an ear in each hand. Except sometimes she doesn't want her ears stroked! Then she makes it very clear, wiggling her head, shaking you off. She meets my eyes with a steady and unflinching gaze, with her odd hyphen-shaped pupils, such as donkeys have.

Initially, our relationship was not easy. She had arrived with lice and I had to bath her—she doesn't like getting wet. It took a year for her to forgive me. She and Susan bonded during that year. She also arrived with a very large belly. We were convinced she must be pregnant. We waited with eager anticipation for the arrival of a baby donkey. Which never arrived. Lina simply had a very large belly.

She will call out if she feels neglected, emitting one of her foghorn cries or the slowly building hee-hee-hee-hee-hee-HAW that sounds like a woman climaxing. Over the years we've had her she has become increasingly integrated into our lives, beloved and petted. She has come to expect such attention. And talking to her has been a large part of that.

Recently Lina has been suffering from abscesses in one front hoof. It is a very painful condition, requiring soaking, poultices, bandaging, and even a course of injections at one stage. There have been several days where she hasn't been able to put her hoof on the ground, which means she has to get around as best she can on three legs. It has meant keeping her locked up because it is not good for the foot to be out in the mud. She has borne all this with incredible fortitude.

Every day as I soaked or bandaged, or as I held her while she was given the injection, I would talk to her, telling her that she was very brave and that we were making it better. I felt like a terrible fraud because it got worse before it got better. She didn't hold this against me but would stand patiently, sometimes snuffling my hair, as I knelt beside her with her foot on my knee. While my words might not have helped the condition, I do believe they helped her cope with it. She felt loved and cared for.

My relationship with Vincent is more complicated than that with Charlie and Lina. I ask nothing of those two but that they be themselves and open their hearts to me as mine has opened to them. But I ride Vincent and he is large and potentially dangerous. Unlike the other two, he is still a mystery to me. But sometimes, just when I am most frustrated with him, he will respond to me in a surprising way. There have been three occasions when I have been feeling either very unwell or very unhappy and then he shows his concern and affection. But often he is a standoffish, cranky bugger.

One evening I went up to the barn and he had his back turned to me and ignored me. I decided to ask him a question *a la* Marta Williams. I stood in front of his stable door, closed my eyes and focused on him and mentally asked: *Vincent, why are you always so cranky?* I didn't even hear him turn around but suddenly he was snuffling at my hair and, it seemed to me, saying with surprise, *I'm not cranky!*

I would have liked to continue the conversation: *So what is it then? Why do you sometimes seem annoyed to see me?* But we got no further.

*

In the 1920s, a Californian writer called J. Allen Boone was given the task of caretaking a German Shepherd named Strongheart, one of the first canine movie stars of the silent film era. Boone became fascinated by the obvious intelligence of the dog—intelligence and wisdom that made Boone feel like he was a bit of an imbecile. He decided to find out what Strongheart thought and felt and what his past life had been like.

The process is described in his 1954 classic, *Kinship with All Life*. Initially, he tried sitting Strongheart down and asking him a series of questions. The dog listened politely for a good length of time but eventually got up and left the room.

While Boone had failed to read Strongheart's mind, he became convinced the dog could read his. An early example presented itself:

Boone decided to take the day off and take Strongheart for one of their favourite outings, a walk in the hills. No sooner had he formulated the thought than Strongheart rushed up to him in great excitement and began bringing the items of clothing he would need from the bedroom—jeans, boots, walking stick—and placed them at his feet.

'How did the dog know that I had changed my plans and was going to take him on an outing? There had been no outward communication between us at all. As a matter of fact, I had not known where he was except in a general way for some hours. In the supposed privacy of my own mind I had suddenly chanted intention, and then he appeared on the scene knowing all about it.'[9]

I suppose I have taken it for granted for a long time that many dogs can read minds. Ours know when I pick up the car keys if it is going to be a journey that involves them or not. They just somehow know. And not just dogs. Vincent, for example, always knows when I am going to take him in the trailer, and is all expectation and nervousness. In his book *Dogs That Know When Their Owners Are Coming Home*, biologist and author Rupert Sheldrake takes the 'mind reader' idea further, believing that telepathy can occur when the pet is not even with its owner, that they can pick up on distress, for example, or find their absent owner in a strange place. He cites many cases of animals showing signs of distress at distant emergencies involving their owners, including one he witnessed while caring for a Labrador named Ruggles for some friends whose son was away skiing in the Italian Alps. Although Ruggles had settled in well, one morning when he returned from a walk at 11.30am, he would not move from the front door. He remained there for hours. Only later did Sheldrake learn that the boy had fallen out of a chairlift, broken his leg and been taken to hospital. The accident happened at 11am.

Sheldrake also documents examples of dogs finding their owners in distant places. In one, an Irish terrier named Prince disappeared from his London home shortly after his soldier owner was posted to France in 1914. Some weeks later, Prince turned up in Armentieres, where he was reunited with his master.

'Such behaviour', he writes, 'cannot be explained in terms of a sense of direction, or at least not a sense of direction that depends on any quality of the destination itself.'

This is in tune with Marta Williams, but she believes we can train ourselves to be 'telepathic' as well.

Like Williams, Boone talks a lot about the need for a human to make a real effort and have real humility if they wish to establish communication with a non-human creature. He wrote of his time with Stongheart: 'Our curriculum was flexible, unpredictable, practical—and full of fun. It was by no means an easy course. I had a large assortment of wrong beliefs about dogs and other animals; these notions had to be cleared out in order to make room for the facts. It took discipline...a sense of wonder and appreciation...inner and outer flexibility.

'I was searching for the universal best in qualities...For qualities of abiding worth. For the kind of qualities that we humans always respect and honor whenever we find them in the members of our own species.'[10]

He equipped himself with a notebook, a book of synonyms and a dictionary, the latter to try to put into words the qualities that he was seeing in the dog.

'I knew that what I was actually being privileged to watch was not a dog expressing great qualities, but rather, great qualities expressing a dog. He was radiating them from deep within himself, flinging them out as freely and lavishly as the sun does its rays. He was not trying in the least to achieve this effect; he was just letting it happen.'[11]

Boone and Strongheart had a favourite place they liked to sit when they reached the mountain top while on one of their walks. It had a fine vista over the countryside below.

'To my amazement Strongheart was not watching anything *below* him at all. His gaze was focussed on a point in the sky considerably above the horizon line. He was staring off into fathomless space. Out there beyond the ability of my human senses to identify what it was, *something* was holding the big dog's attention like a magnet! And it was giving him great satisfaction, great contentment, great peace of mind. That fact was not only written all over him; it was permeating the atmosphere like a perfume.'[12]

How strongly this reminds me of Vincent! Of the way he gazes from his stable window over the gullies and bushland towards the great escarpment. He has that same quality of intense concentration and intense contentment. An air of satisfaction. And he, too, seems not to be gazing at anything specific but rather beyond the horizon.

As Boone sat there watching the dog in front of him gazing out into the wide blue yonder, he began questioning him silently, a whole series of penetrating questions about his life, but silently, not verbally as he had before. When his store of questions ran out, Boone just sat there, not expecting anything: 'I relaxed into a pleasing feeling of suspended animation and a blank state of mind'.

Then the dog turned and stared at him, stared and stared with X-ray eyes. He realised the dog was talking to him silently. Then the dog looked away, and presently Boone discovered that he had answers to the questions he had asked, answers that were subsequently verified.

*

Dogs are the only species that have fuller communication with another species—humans—than with their own kind. The extraordinary fidelity that a dog displays towards their human companion can extend even to the grave. Rupert Sheldrake tells a story about the attachment of a dog to his owner's body. In Austria, a farm dog called Sultan lost his master when the master was taken suddenly ill, rushed to hospital and later died. The master's body was buried in a graveyard some five kilometres from the farm, in an area where Sultan had never been. A few weeks after the burial, Sultan disappeared from the farm. Eventually, an acquaintance who lived near the graveyard told the family that he had seen Sultan lying on the farmer's grave.

How did Sultan know where his old companion was buried when it was such a distance and not somewhere he had ever been? Sheldrake asks how Sultan could have known about bodies being buried in graves at all. But that part does not surprise me—most farm dogs will know about the bodies of dead creatures being in the earth. They observe what goes on around them, as we do. But what is surprising is the way he was able to *find* the grave. What sense led him to that particular plot of earth? Smell only, or something else? Some other sense, a sixth sense, that we are not privy to? Or is it simply intuition, which many of us have in a small dose and which they have in spades?

In her work as an animal communicator, Marta Williams is often called upon to find lost animals. And she is very often successful. She 'tunes in' to them and visualises where they may be. Perhaps that is what Sultan did—the fact that his master was no longer alive may not have stopped his ability to sense his whereabouts.

In one of her more confronting beliefs, Williams thinks it is possible for humans, too, to communicate with animal companions that have died. In its way, this is a kind of clairvoyance, which, as she says, simply means 'clear seeing'.

Perhaps most of us have blocked our seeing with prejudice. Refusing to see our commonality with the animals that share our lives, we walk among them with blinkers on. Generations of censored logic and arrogance—our human-centred view of the world—may have led us to lose faculties that other creatures have retained.

Chapter 3
Through a New Lens

When I was about ten years old my family took a long trip through the outback, travelling up through western Queensland to the Northern Territory. We travelled in a VW Kombi and in addition to my parents, myself and my sister Jenny, there was our dog Brutus, a beautiful and loyal chap. Brutus was a rare and, as it turned out, prized cattle dog known as a Smithfield heeler. He was rather better looking than the average cattle dog but he had never worked cattle in his life. His job was to look after us, and he took it seriously. He never strayed and always slept underneath the van.

But one morning we woke at our campsite a few miles outside the little town of Julia Creek to find that Brutus had disappeared. We waited for him, then drove into the town to look for him, then drove back out to the campsite beside the long red corrugated road. All day we did this, back and forth, examining every corner of the small town, then rushing back to where we had camped in case he returned. We were all distressed by his disappearance. In the late afternoon as the sun began to sink we were just about to give up. We heaped the cold ashes on the fire and removed all trace of our campsite. Then, just as we were getting into the van, there he was, coming towards us, trotting unevenly down that long dirt road. He flopped at our feet, grinning up at us, tongue lolling. Then we saw his feet. The pads on all four paws were red raw and bleeding. He started to lick them.

We picked him up and put him in the van, and with relief and joy headed on our way. Brutus could not tell us what had happened to him but we knew that wherever he had been, it was not of his choosing. For three days he did nothing but sleep and lick his sore paws. How far he must have travelled to get back to us! And he found us—that was the remarkable thing. Found the tiny dot of the campsite where we'd only stopped overnight. He didn't get sidetracked by the sights and smells of the town but came back to us. How many miles he travelled we never knew. We kept him close after that, and he showed even less inclination to leave our sides.

*

When Vincent arrived at the farm four years ago he was calm and easy to handle and not bad-tempered. But he was not entirely reliable either. For the first six months, I never handled him without putting a head-collar on him first, even in the stable. I had to learn to trust him. And he, I realise now, had to learn to trust me, too.

The first time I became aware that he had come to depend on me was about ten months after I got him. We were away, at a strange place, and he'd been sharing a paddock with a horse that he had come to like. But the property had been sold and the whole place was in a state of flux. When his paddock mate was moved to another property, Vincent became very distressed, rushing about the paddock, whinnying pathetically. There were other horses in nearby paddocks but they were no consolation to him. When I arrived, he came and stood in front of me and put his head down so his nose was on my boots and his forehead was against my knees. He was literally asking to be comforted. I rubbed and pulled his ears. Ever since, that has been one of his favourite things.

This period of distress, which went on for days but felt like weeks, was a revelation for me, too. I was amazed at how distressed I became at his distress. Like a pair of co-dependants, we exacerbated each other's anxiety. Within a few days, I found a new place for him to stay. It was safe and calm and there were other horses close around him. He settled immediately; we both relaxed.

It is said that a horse taken from the herd feels like it is dying. And I could see that in Vincent. Left on his own, he was mortally afraid. As soon as he had company and a secure environment, he felt safe. As if safety is his No. 1 need.

In an unfamiliar environment, another horse can provide that sense of security, which is why most horses are much better when ridden out in the company of another horse. When an environment feels safe and familiar, the company of another horse is not so crucial. For example, when a group of horses are grazing in a paddock, one horse may wander off and be out of sight of the others yet happily eating. It feels safe; it knows this paddock.

These days I handle Vincent easily without a head-collar. I mess about with him in the stable, brush him, put on his boots, change his rugs. If I do this in a mechanical way—offhand or hurriedly—he just ignores me. Lets me get on with it but doesn't really engage. But if I go into his stable just to talk to him, to have a little commune, he'll come over of his own accord after a bit, and enjoy a rub between the eyes or having his ears pulled.

I don't always know why he responds the way he does. Maybe if I can find out more about what he feels, I'll better understand. That goes for all the animals. We only have our own emotions to work with in trying to understand theirs. Perhaps they have a whole different vocabulary of feelings, just as different languages don't always have words that exactly correlate. If people from different cultures don't have identical responses, how can we expect feelings to exactly correlate between species? Yet feel they do. And by watching closely I hope to see what they feel, even if I can only use the paltry instrument of our own language to describe what I see.

*

What do I see in a donkey, the very decided Miss Lina? Curiosity and irritation, affection and stubbornness. Resignation and sadness sometimes. Perkiness at other times.

In Vincent, I sometimes see nervousness and anxiety, satisfaction when he knows he has worked well, happiness when he's released into the paddock and can kick up his heels, bossiness sometimes (with Lina), and often a calm acceptance of my company.

Then there is the mare, Chelsea. Chelsea belongs to Jan, who has lived in the cottage on our place almost as long as we have. Jan has been around so long she is family. Her mare Chelsea is different from both Vincent and Lina. She is sweet-natured but also high-spirited, jealous, nervy and temperamental.

Even the chooks show their feelings. I can see when they are alarmed, when they are indignant, and when they are content. And I can see how they have established their pecking order. This is hardly democratic but a pecking order is the way chickens establish and maintain control, social organisation and ultimately the flock's survival. The strongest, most aggressive chicken pecks its way to power with its pointy beak. Occasionally blood is drawn, and even a fight to the death can result.

The chook at the top gets first access to food, water and other resources, such as the best nesting and roosting spot. And so he or she becomes even stronger and healthier. In return, the chook-in-chief is responsible for watching out for predators, ushering the flock to safety and finding food.

The introduction of a new chicken or chickens can upset the pecking order and fights can result as a new order is established. But if a chicken becomes injured and bleeds in such a fight, the other chickens are liable to turn on it, peck it to death and eat it.

Jostling for a place in the pecking order begins early. Skirmishes and play fights can get underway in chicks just a few days old, with more aggressive pecking at about six weeks. If a flock contains a rooster, he is nearly always top of the pecking order.

Occasionally bullying results in a flock when a member does not know their place. Usually the bullies are in the middle rank and they make the lives of those lower down the pecking order miserable by pecking, pulling out their feathers, blocking access to food or following another member. Separating the bully for a few days can solve the problem. When returned to the flock, the chicken is considered a new member and has to find their place in the pecking order.

The pecking order isn't static and changes each time a chicken dies. This rearrangement will be most dramatic if a senior chicken dies, less so if the creature is lower down the pecking order.

*

Something has been stealing eggs from the chook pen. Possibly a rat, or maybe a snake, knocking a large hole in an egg every day and draining the contents. The chooks are fairly quiet creatures, with a bit of clucking and a rare squawk, but two things can make them really call out. One is the triumphant laying of an egg; the other is when an alien creature invades their pen. Triumph (I can't call it anything else—imagine it, an egg the size of your head, every day!) and fear.

Mostly the chooks lay their eggs in the laying boxes as required. But at certain times they will find a well-hidden spot in their day yard and start laying them there. Hiding them from the humans who come each day and take their precious eggs away. When they get enough, they will go clucky and sit on them. They have been hoarding their eggs to breed.

How do they know to hide their eggs at these times and not at others? When I find them, and take the eggs from under a clucky chook (they are not fertile but she doesn't know that), she squawks at me with undisguised anger. At other times, being told to move elicits mere indignation.

Am I being anthropomorphic in attributing indignation to hens and calculating thought to a donkey, pleasure to Vincent and high spirits to the mare? Anthropomorphism, of course, in some circles is a sin. But it's a worse sin to think they are insentient, less 'evolved' than us, so it doesn't matter how we treat them.

What we believe about animal self-awareness is one of the determinants of how we treat them, or how we feel *entitled* to treat them. If they do not feel pain, if they are not self-aware, if they are not rational, if they don't have emotions…if, in other words, they are not like us, we feel entitled to treat them without consideration.

I've spent my entire life around animals but I feel as if, for the first time, I am permitting myself to explore areas that have been always central to me but kept peripheral to my intellectual self.

Chapter 4
Farm Animals and Ethics

Keil-na-nain was already set up for cattle when we bought it, with a small set of stockyards and water troughs in each of the three main paddocks. We grazed a handful of steers each year, mostly to keep the grass down in summer. Come each winter, we'd have to decide whether to hand-feed them through the cold months or sell them. The decision often came down to the condition of the steers—whether they were big enough to go to market—or the condition of the paddocks.

A few years ago we bought thirty acres next door. It has given us more options. Now, instead of just fattening a handful of steers, we can run a small herd of cows and their calves. The matriarch of the herd, the dominant cow, is Freckle, so called because she has a brown spot on the cheek of her otherwise white face. One of the reasons we bought Herefords is because they often have distinctive markings, so one can tell them apart. Our cows are what is known as Poll Herefords, which means they don't have horns.

At present, there are seven young calves and we enjoy watching them, particularly at dusk when they frisk and frolic together. They are all pretty at this age even though some may grow up to be no great beauties. They are curious, too, and will approach people much more readily than their mothers do. One little fellow is a ring-in—his brothers and sisters are pure Poll Hereford but this one was fathered by the neighbour's bull that got through the fence. The cross-bred calf is chocolate brown with a white blaze. He is his mother's first calf and she is very protective of him, always running after him when he wanders. He takes little notice, goes where he pleases, investigates things and people, and is always curious. We have broken our usual rule about not naming the male calves and called him Bert, because, I suppose, he is distinctive in both his looks and his behaviour. He is a little individual.

But the cows and calves are not pets. When you have a farm, and worry about such things, you strike an uneasy bargain with yourself. You may have a favourite cow who you will spend extra money on for a vet. You may get to know her well because you might have her for quite a few years. You may give her and some of the other cows names. But the male calves you don't name because from the day they are born, you know what their fate will be—sooner or later they'll be off to market and off to the butchers. And so it will be with Bert when he is a couple of years old.

One of the heifers had her leg broken when she was only a few hours old. Her mother, another novice, trod on her. If we were serious farmers that would probably have been the end of the calf. But we called in the vet, who made a cast. She got around quite well in her cast so we named her Peggy Sue. The leg healed and now you would never know she had broken it. She is a very independent and rather pushy young thing. Just like her mother. Like her mother at her age, she will drink from any handy cow, if the cow will let her. At only a couple of months, she also eats hay like an old hand. This is a heifer that had a rocky start but will get on. Did she inherit her resilience from her mother or was it because of that broken leg?

Now that all, bar one, have a baby, our small herd of cows have bonded like a family. One cow minds the calves while the others graze. It's not unusual to see a cow licking a calf that is not her own. Each day I give them hay and stand among them and they are more relaxed with me than they have ever been before. It is almost as if I am a member of the family.

*

In *The Pig Who Sang to the Moon*, author Jeffrey Masson, a psychoanalyst and former research chief of the Sigmund Freud Archives, looks at the lives and emotional responses of farm animals. His is a radical view that sees husbanding of farm animals for food as wrong—even milking cows and keeping chooks for eggs. He is mainly concerned with the large-scale enterprises: the enormous and miserable chicken farms; the cows who lose their calves almost as soon as they are born so they can be milked. He talks of the relentless misery of sheep, the death sentences hanging over steers.

As he told Salon Magazine: 'I feel that it's not ours to take. The milk is there for a calf, not for a human. We're the only species that drinks the milk of another species...There is no animal domesticated today who gets to live out his or her full life span. It just doesn't happen, because there is no money in that, and they are there to answer our needs. It's an economic deal that we make with ourselves, not with them. It's not a contract with the animals.'[13]

He is right about the large-scale operations where the animals are just a tool to produce something that can be sold and where they do live miserable lives. But he paints with too broad a brush. There surely is a middle way between humans living off the cruel practices of agribusiness and everyone becoming vegan?

But maybe what I do here with our handful of cows is just a salve to my conscience. I eat meat and look out at the pleasant lives our steers live for a couple of years and like to think the meat I am eating is coming from cattle who enjoyed a similar existence. I am fooling myself. Is it enough to eat free-range chickens and free-range pork and hope the beef cattle that were my steak had a nice life?

To live so conscious of what it is we are living off would be almost unbearable. It might mean eschewing woollen clothing because sheep must find being shorn an uncomfortable experience. On the other hand, maybe it is a relief to the sheep to lose that heavy overcoat of wool, to move freely, unburdened. A merino fleece can weigh ten kilos or more when it's dry, and a lot more when the weather is wet. Is being shorn any worse than going to the dentist?

Masson believes we do not have the right to use animals for our own purposes. But farm animals have been domesticated for thousands of years. Releasing them to fend for themselves is no solution. Anyone who has seen animals escape from their enclosure knows the startled, even haunted, look they have as they try to find safety. We are responsible for what they have become, and because of that we have to remain responsible for their care and safety.

Masson praises the sanctuaries that take in abused or neglected animals. These animals are given good living conditions; they aren't left to fend for themselves. For farm animals, the best life is when they can live in herds in open fields and be allowed a good long life. But does that mean we shouldn't eat them?

Peter Singer's position is that eating animals is okay if they have had a good life up to that point and if the killing is done humanely. Masson says animals know when they are going to be slaughtered and so there is no such thing as a humane killing. All animals want to live, and he gives some examples of the grand and celebrated escapes of several animals who got away on their way to the abattoir.

Occasionally such episodes capture international media attention. This was the case when a pair of pigs escaped while being offloaded at a Wiltshire abattoir in Britain. Dubbed Butch and Sundance—after the wild west outlaws—they were on the run for a week. After their recapture, they spent the rest of their lives at an animal sanctuary in Kent. The BBC even produced a drama based on their tale. Heartwarming as such a tale may be, the reality is that billions of animals are killed for food each year.

Millions of animals are killed to feed millions of people. Can we say 'no' to that and how would the world look if we did? What would happen to the cattle and sheep, the camels and goats? If they were not kept to provide food, would they be kept at all? Some perhaps, but very few in the overall scheme of things. The relationships that humans have with these animals are because we farm them.

Even here, on our small acreage, I have to make decisions about their future lives all the time: how many can we feed? Do we have enough fodder to last through the winter? How long can the steers be kept? If we decide not to breed any more, what do I do with our young bull Bill?

We can retire the cows, say 'No more babies for you', give them a nice retirement and let them die a natural death. But I suspect I will go on eating meat. I will have distanced myself from the problem. At least now I am a little complicit, am forced to think of these things, am forced to live with the consequences.

Chapter 5
Animals in the Dock

To say that farm animals become habituated to their living arrangements is not to say they don't have feelings. Perhaps they become habituated *because* they have feelings. Like us, they construct their day around the known, around routines that provide a sense of comfort and security.

This last week, Vincent has been away and the other horses have been given a different routine. Let them just be horses (and donkey), we said, and put them onto the hill paddock above the house. They haven't been locked up at night, have been left unrugged (the weather has been good), and generally have had more 'freedom' than usual. I don't think they particularly like it. Yesterday Chelsea cantered up to me while I was walking near them. She was restless and started heading off ahead of me towards the barn and the usual horse paddocks as if she wanted to get back there. The old gelding, Jim, meanwhile, is looking a bit feral—he has rubbed bits of hair off and his coat has lost its usual gloss. Donkey is just bored and a bit put out.

If we leave them there for a few weeks they will adjust; will stop looking for us (and their evening feed) of an afternoon; will perhaps even become a little skittish and avoid us. The bonds between us will weaken as they learn to live on their own, as they see less of us, and are not groomed or petted. In which case, I say, what's the point of having them? We have them because we love them and enjoy being with them. Yes, they can get by without us, provided they have grass and water. Am I being anthropocentric in believing that their lives are a little poorer, too, without *our* company?

*

Animal trainer Steve Jefferys is best known for kicking off the Sydney Olympics when he galloped into the stadium on his horse Ammo, like *The Man from Snowy River*. Jefferys believes that in working with dogs and horses one should treat them as one would another person. Watching him with his animals you can see the almost conversational way in which he interacts with them. For him, trust and respect are part of the equation.

But to hardline animal behaviourists, this idea is abhorrent. Another trainer, Australian Andrew McLean, who works with horses and elephants, does not believe the term 'respect' is appropriate to apply or expect from a relationship with an animal. An animal might learn to react to a signal from a human but that has nothing to do with respect: it is about learning, teaching the required response through a combination of pressure and reward.

In McLean's view, applying anthropomorphic concepts like 'respect' is not in the animal's best interests because it can lead people to believe that an animal has a greater sense of intention, or purpose, than it does in fact have. People end up saying an animal is 'bad' when it doesn't do what they want, whereas probably it is simply that the person has not made it clear to the animal exactly what is required.

'I try to teach riders that a lazy horse is not a personality disorder; it is actually a learned response. Sure, horses come to us with different genetic predispositions, but the outcomes are something we can change,' McLean says.[14]

To burden animals with the responsibility for their actions is reminiscent of medieval and pre-modern Europe, when animals were quite regularly tried before courts if they were believed to have committed a 'crime' against humans. A huge range of creatures was so tried: pigs appear to have been the chief 'offenders', but also oxen, goats, horses, dogs, rats, and even ants and flies. Several hundred cases have been documented, most of them occurring between the fifteenth and seventeenth centuries.

In 1386, a tribunal in Normandy sentenced a sow to be mangled, maimed in the head and forelegs and then hanged after it tore off the face and arms of a child, who died as a result. This was retributive eye-for-an-eye justice for the creature's actions. The sow was dressed in human clothes and executed in the public square in the town of Falaise. A fresco of the execution was painted on a wall of the local church, since whitewashed.[15]

It's possible Shakespeare was aware of the capital punishment of animals. In *The Merchant of Venice*, Shylock's most vocal critic, Gratiano, attacks him thus: 'Thy currish spirit/ Governed a wolf who, hanged for human slaughter/ Even from the gallows did his fell soul fleet'.

Some animal trials verged on farce, such as the rats accused of destroying a village's barley crop in sixteenth-century France. Ordered to appear in court the rodents failed to show up. Their lawyer, Bartholomew Chassenée, successfully argued that, because there were so many rats involved over such a wide area, they could not all have been notified of their day in court. When the rats failed to turn up to a later date, the lawyer asserted they could not safely do so since they would have encountered cats, their mortal enemies, en route. A Hollywood movie, *The Hour of the Pig*, starring Colin Firth, was based on the celebrated lawyer's life.

From a cock burned at the stake for the 'crime' of laying an egg, to a colony of termites ordered to move house because they were undermining the foundations of a monastery, or a hive of bees convicted of homicide, the thinking appears to have been that if a crime occurred then it was incumbent that blame be attached to some animate (or even inanimate) being – thinking that persists in some traditional societies.

Some people might see this as another example of human abuse of animals—a bizarre anthropomorphism whereby animals are seen as capable of committing crimes against humans. And it does seem bizarre. But what occurs to me is that a pig who ate a child would certainly not receive the courtesy of a trial these days: it would be immediately killed. Similarly with a vicious dog.

The earliest known trials date from the seventh century and involve excommunication by ecclesiastical courts. Moles, locusts and serpents were among the first creatures to attract the attention of these courts. During this period early Christianity was gradually overtaking and superimposing itself on societies where animism had previously dominated, where it was widely believed that all creatures had souls and were capable of being inhabited by spirits and demons. Given this holistic mind-frame, it is not so surprising that animals were treated as co-believers and were called to account before the courts, much as a human would be.

In the thirteenth century, the influential Italian priest, philosopher and theologian Thomas Aquinas said that the only possible justification for punishing animals was that they were the agents of Satan; that they had been taken over by Satan and used by him, because otherwise beasts were either God's creatures and not to be cursed or mere brutes, in which cases legal sanction would be pointless. Seeing animals as agents of Satan does help explain why they may have been tried; it puts them on a par with witches. Women accused of being witches were also doing the devil's work, in the eyes of those who accused them. Like animals, women's lives have historically been controlled by the men who 'owned' them.

But exactly why animals had the right to a trial is still not clear. If they were so lowly, why bother? In 1666 an ecclesiastical court in Berne found that 'an ox is created for man's sake, and can therefore be killed for his sake'.

It seems possible that the prosecution of animals was part of a slow and awkward transition out of animism, part of that process whereby

47

the Christian church moved its followers away from their pagan, holistic ways to an acceptance of the hierarchy insisted on by the church. Animals were no longer companions and familiars. They must be subject to the laws of the church and the secular courts. It is hard to ascertain whether it was common for the accused animal to be found not guilty. Although there was a fourteenth-century case where a sow was convicted of killing a child, but her six piglets were acquitted because of their youth!

The punishments varied: sometimes a rap on the head, other times a formal curse, and sometimes a full and sombre execution complete with a hangman.

The medieval trials gave animals credit for being individuals with individual agency. They recognised the life trajectory of the animal and that it could not be disrupted by man without cause or proof (however flimsy and manufactured). While on one level such trials could be seen as abusing animals for acts they could not be blamed for, on another it was offering a degree of respect. Animals could not be killed without justification. (Leaving aside for a moment that they were killed for food all the time.)

As 'rational man' came to the fore at the end of the medieval age, this ceased to be the case. Man ruled the roost and animals ceased to be given credit for anything very much. Certainly not with having souls. Ultimately they became nothing more than property.

Animal trials appear to have been far less common in Britain than in mainland Europe, especially France and Switzerland. Instead, from the early thirteenth century, the practice developed of holding the owner of the animal responsible for its transgressions. Thus animals became caught up in the English fondness for building its legal system around questions of property and ownership.

*

So it was that several centuries later I found myself in Maitland Magistrates Court, charged with having an uncontrollable dog. The dog in question was Scruffy. Scruffy was a lovable mutt who turned up in my front yard when he was less than a year old. He had a finely chiselled head with whiskers and shaggy eyebrows that hung over deep chocolate eyes. His body was solid but longish. And he had ridiculously short legs and no tail. He was a terrier crossed with just about everything.

He was a sociable dog and didn't like to stay home alone. So he'd go into town and visit the shops—he had a regular route and became well known. And he was almost always back by the time I got home, although I did once get a call from a shopkeeper to say that Scruffy was lying on her carpet and didn't want to go home because it was raining outside and would I come and get him. He never caused any trouble, but inevitably he fell foul of the local dog catcher. After the third time I bailed him out of the pound, a summons came in the mail.

I was required to appear; Scruffy was not. But I took him anyway and left him tied up outside. Luckily, by the time the court date came around Scruffy and I had moved. I could honestly tell the magistrate that Scruffy was now living in Sydney and in a securely fenced yard; he would cause no further angst for the Maitland dog catcher.

I was given a fine and a lecture about the Dog Act. I left contrite and went outside to find Scruffy surrounded by adoring friends. He turned and grinned up at me with what I called his Marilyn Monroe look—looking over his shoulder with a smile that was both coy and flirtatious, and utterly irresistible, the same smile he'd been using for years on the Maitland shopkeepers.

*

When I was growing up on the semi-urban, semi-rural fringes of the city, both kids and dogs were accustomed to running free. It was an area of raw streets and empty blocks and slabs of remnant bushland, of old mulberry trees in the backyards of former farmhouses, and creeks where tadpoles could be caught. But slowly suburbia was engulfing us; tarmac and kerb and guttering and 'The Sewer'. No more would we hear the footsteps of the night-soil men, the murmuring voices and the *swish* as they brushed past shrubs on the way to backyard dunnies. With urbanisation, the marauding attacks by the dog catcher intensified. All the local dogs knew the dog catcher's van. As soon as he turned into the street, they'd scuttle off behind the houses, seeking safety in the backyards that they normally eschewed. The kids would join in, running up and down the street calling, 'Dog catcher! Dog catcher!'

And the parents would emerge to make sure their mutt was out of sight. Woe betide the pooch that had gone only as far as its front yard. If there was no fence the dog catcher might well still swoop. And then there'd be an altercation between the homeowner and dog catcher, which we kids delighted in. We were an anti-authoritarian lot and the dogs apparently took their cue from us.

We never thought the dogs might be better off in the RSPCA pound than roaming the streets—maybe because there were fewer cars on the road so the risk of a dog being run over was lower. The RSPCA was in the next road along, but rather than seeing this as a worthy institution doing good works, we viewed it as a prison and occasionally toyed with the idea of a mass breakout.

The dogs were loyal to their human pack and generally the humans were loyal to their dogs. It was no surprise to anyone that the dogs could recognise the dog catcher's van or that they knew which houses were safe harbours in an emergency. As well as loyalty, the dogs displayed fear and affection, cunning sometimes, joy often, and guilt frequently. They could be tender and sympathetic, or fierce and combative. Some dogs were more regularly the former and some the latter. If you had told their owners that they were anthropomorphising their dogs, they wouldn't have known what you were talking about, and wouldn't have believed you if they did. Those who live closely with animals have no trouble recognising their qualities.

Chapter 6
The Company of Cats

'When she is young, she is frolicsome and active, and as she grows up, nimble, dexterous, cleanly, and insinuating. It is true that she is somewhat of a flattering thief, possessing address, subtlety, and the desire of plunder; that she knows how to conceal her steps, and her designs; to watch for opportunities to seize her prey; to fly from pursuit, and remain at a distance until solicited to return. But then she has many respectable qualities; she is gay and vivacious, attached to the roof that shelters her, and will rarely quit it, even for a more commodious home.' So wrote the anonymous author of *Domesticated Animals; Considered with reference to Civilization and the Arts*.[16]

Any cat lover can identify with this description. And any cat lover who has ever been miserable knows the comfort a cat can give. They are not as responsive as a dog—they won't look at you beseechingly or whine sympathetically as you sob. But they are very *there*, both self-contained (in a reassuring sort of way) and companionable. They are so physically huggable, like living teddies, but they also set an example if their humans care to see it. They will purr and offer condolences but they also seem to say: *Be as I am in the world—look for comfort, look for kindness, but most of all look after No. 1.*

The sound of a cat purring on your lap is comforting. But what does it mean for the cat? Why do cats purr? The answer is not simple. It may be an expression of pleasure, certainly, and of establishing or restoring harmony. A kitten learns about purring at its mother's teat.

The little one suckles, the mother purrs, and the milk flows. The little ones, too, start to purr when very young.

Kittens begin purring when just a couple of days old, which likely lets their mothers find them at feeding time. The offspring are not simply imitating their purring mothers, since kittens are born deaf (and blind).

But an older cat will often purr in unusual situations. I've often seen a cat, after being chastised by its human, try to re-establish a rapport and harmony by purring. Also, a cat in a slightly threatening situation—being observed closely by the family dog, for example—will sometimes crouch and purr, as if to say, *Come on, we're all friends here.*

Although it often seems the cat is purring for our benefit, that is not the way of cats at all. Yes, he may be comfortable, all is right in his world, you are paying him the attention that, at this moment, he wants. So he purrs. But I've also noticed that if my cat is keeping me company when I am unwell, he will often have that motor running at full bore as if attempting to set the world to rights for both of us.

Scientists used to think purring was the sound of blood surging through a large vein that carries blood from the lower half of the body into the heart. More recently, purring is believed to emanate from a cat's larynx. When cats breathe, they dilate and constrict the area around their vocal cords, the air around the larynx vibrates and the result is a purr. Purring is distinct from other cat sounds in that it is produced during the whole respiratory cycle—during inhaling and exhaling. Other sounds, such as a 'meow', are produced only on exhalation. Purring is thought to be part voluntary, part instinctive.

Some cats purr a little, others a lot. But why do they purr? What function does this rhythmic sound serve? Science still isn't sure; purring remains a puzzle. Far less research has been undertaken on cat behaviour and communication than on dogs. The ability to purr appears to be limited to smaller cats such as domestic cats, bobcats, cougars and lynxes. Big cats—lions, tigers, leopards and jaguars—can roar but not purr.

Cats can purr when they are in pain, possibly as a way to soothe themselves. Research suggests that the vibrations from purring can help them heal after injury or stress. One study found that some cats purr at frequencies optimal for pain relief and bone repair.[17]

It's often quipped that dogs have owners and cats have staff. Cats aren't above manipulating their humans. All cat owners know that loud, relentless purr when puss wants to be fed. Research has found that cats can hide within their purr a plaintive and urgent cry—including when trying to solicit food—which is similar to the sound frequency of a human baby crying. It is thought this sound may trigger in humans a nurturing instinct and a desire to respond.[18] Cats are not concerned with ambition; they have no work ethic. They are not ashamed of sleeping the day away. Rarely does one find a creature so at ease with itself and with its world. Do they have a moral sense? They can be taught right from wrong. And I see signs of a sense of justice: they know what is due to them, and they know to whom they must defer. They certainly exhibit jealousy and are territorial. Female cats are the most caring of mothers, and indeed will mother those not their own.

But why do we love them so? Is it the softness of their fur, their elegance and beauty? Or is it the ease of them? Their loyalty and calm presence? They are individuals and express themselves, in their own way. Perhaps it is that they require so little of us while giving constancy and a sense of attachment.

Their home is their world, and they are so comfortable in it that they help to make us so. Above all, they are good company. Mostly a cat is content to sit near us, and sometimes look at us, and sometimes purr and sometimes come up for a scratch or a cuddle. I suspect that, for a surprising number of people, a cat is the living creature they are closest to. Cats will thrive in a family, but they are a single person's companion par excellence, particularly if that person is elderly or can't get out much.

They make few demands, only to be fed, and will look at you with an open, unjudging gaze that implies equality. Maybe it is this that makes them such excellent companions. Not for a cat the fawning obsequiousness that a dog often displays. You and your cat exist on equal terms in her world. And perhaps that is why one never feels truly alone when you have a cat.

A cat relates to its humans much as a kitten relates to its mother, and can continue to display very kittenish behaviour—chasing their tail, playing with things, running and leaping—into old age. But when not being 'kittenish', most adult cats display a sober and reflective mien. Whether they are actually reflective is another matter.

People get not just pleasure from owning a cat (or a dog), but it can also be good for their health: pet owners live longer than people who don't have pets. Stroking a cat is a stress-buster and helps lower blood pressure.

Over several months, our cat Charlie has turned into one of those stress-busting cats. Initially he was anything but. Initially he was too active, too *interactive*. When he sat on your lap he immediately started paw-pawing at you, and not just in that gentle way that is meant to be leftover from the days when a kitten kneaded its mother's belly to make the milk flow. No, Charlie's kneading was more the sort that a tomcat uses when he wants to hold down a female. Humping.

After his hormones settled down, about eight weeks after he was neutered, he started to ease off on the humping. Now he hardly ever does it. Now if I am lying on the couch he will drape himself along my torso, a lovely live warm pillow. And he'll purr gently or simply sleep, happy to be stroked. He often *asks* for a stroke, reaching his head up towards one's hand, and opening his mouth a little in the process.

If someone were to say to me 'what is Charlie?', I can give a whole anthropomorphic list. I can also tell you that he is a creature with appetites and emotions; he is a creature with his own unique character; he is aware of the life around him and his place in it; he has fears and habits; he is a creature who has made his home with us, and this is his home as much as it is ours. He is a creature for whom home is important.

Last night, on the news, a woman who works at an animal shelter said it was the adult stray cats that made wonderful companions because they had known human company and lost it. And they were so grateful to have a loving home again that they were perfect pets. That is our experience with Charlie. He wants to be a part of whatever is going on with us. He doesn't seem to accept that as a cat he should have his own routines and own life; he wants to be part of *our* life. Whatever is going on, he's never far away: a walk around the farm, lunch in the garden with friends, cleaning out a cupboard, searching for something in the car, going to the bathroom. There is no such thing as privacy with Charlie—he is always there.

But I'm conscious of how cats are said to live double lives: the quiet homebody, who couldn't even be bothered raising her head from the couch to look at the bird outside the window, who can turn into a screeching fighter or ruthless hunter when away from human company. We can never know what goes on between them when we are not around. Their behaviour can be observed but not their feelings or their subtle communications.

Charlie's confidence has grown markedly in recent months. And rather than sleeping peaceably on the back porch as he did, he now is intent on destroying the cat door. He has learnt to open it, which requires the tricky turning of a knob, not once but twice. He has also, on several occasions, completely pulled the frame of the cat door off its casing. I've heard him do this and it makes an unholy racket, accompanied on more than one occasion by loud cat screams when he gets a paw caught. This doesn't seem to deter him.

It happened last night, brought on because we'd put him out on the porch before the television was turned off and while we were still in the lounge room. Susan went out to reprimand him. She shouted at him as if he were a dog and ordered him into his bed. He did eventually get into the bed but didn't stay there—he got out and glared at her, not cowered at all.

I put the cat door back together again, made sure the big pot plant was blocking his escape on the outside and left him to it. No sooner were we back inside than I heard loud scratching noises as he dug in his litter tray.

'That's why he wanted to get out,' I said.

'But I took him out just a while ago!' Susan said, exasperated. His behaviour brought up several questions. Why is it that you can't order a cat about the way you can order a dog? *Go away, Sit, Get in your bed*. Cats don't much care for commands. A shout and loud clapping of the hands will scare them off—off the kitchen bench, for example. But a cat does not take to instruction.

And why didn't he take the opportunity to defecate when he was outside only minutes before? He had ample opportunity. A cat wants to do what it wants to do when it wants to do it. And that is the beginning and the end of the matter.

Two months after last year's bushfires, dogs and particularly cats were still being found and reunited with their owners. The extent to which people consider cats and dogs to be part of their family was clear in the news reports of the 'refugee camps' where survivors lived in the days and weeks following the fires. Many people could be seen leading or carrying their pet; often they escaped with nothing but their pet. But to even call them 'pets' in this case seems to trivialise the relationship. These fellow animals are part of the family and most people would not have dreamt of leaving them behind. Those who were forced to, or who were away from home when the fires hit, were distraught about it. Some people died trying to save their animals, including two teenage girls who were killed while moving their horses to safety.

*

Many of the 25 per cent of Australians who live alone would be totally alone if not for the company of a cat or dog. It is no small thing. Such people are sharing their lives with another living creature, a creature that cannot tell them (as another human would) if they are happy with their lot or would like to negotiate a different way of doing things around the house. Taking on a relationship with another animal, one that is inarticulate and dependent yet often completely engrossed in and fascinated by you, is a far more complex process than most people realise.

Years ago a friend said to me that she couldn't have a dog because she couldn't bear the way that a dog looked at you, the intensity of the devotion. At the time I found this a strange and amusing comment but I begin to understand what she meant. Inspiring devotion might be nice for the ego but it can also be a terrible burden. It is not only the responsibility—there can also be a sinking feeling that perhaps you are not worthy, that you will be proved wanting. That the animal will be able to see through you.

Chapter 7
Friendships Across Species

Just how much consideration do you give an animal? Mark Rowlands, in his book *The Philosopher and the Wolf*, describes how, as a young academic in Alabama, he bought a wolf cub named Brenin. For more than a decade, the philosopher and Brenin were a pack; their first (and, for a time, their only) loyalty was to one another, as Brenin attended classes and went running with Rowlands and on road trips. Rowlands is neither proud nor ashamed of this deep connection but sees it as almost inevitable. Forming an unbreakable bond with such a strong, awe-inspiring animal is a unique experience, irreplaceable. Rowlands found that the qualities embodied in the wolf outshone most human qualities—there was something cold and pure, uncompromising, about the wolf that seemed to him far superior to the deceiving, manipulative behaviour typical of many human-to-human interactions. We are apes, he says, and it isn't complimentary. For him, the lupine outshines the simian any day.

'There are no wolf-Einsteins, no wolf-Mozarts and no wolf-Shakespeares,' he writes. 'But we have to remember where all this came from. Our scientific and artistic intelligence is a by-product of our social intelligence. And our social intelligence consists in our ability to scheme and deceive more than we are the victim of schemes and deception.'[19]

In the course of his life with the wolf, and reflecting on it after Brenin's death, Rowlands poses questions about the nature of a wolf and the nature of humans. A wolf is not always hankering after something the way that humans hanker for the things they believe might bring happiness. Humans are obsessed with feelings, and always beset by what has gone before and what may come in the future. A human's life is like an arrow, a straight line moving through space, whereas he suspects a wolf's is more like a circle, where the familiar recurs and recurs in a way that would drive most humans berserk. The wolf, and dogs for that matter, seem to genuinely exist in the moment, something Rowlands believes humans are incapable of.

In his life with Brenin, he comes to a conclusion about what it is that creates meaning in a life. He suspects it is when we are most wolf-like, when the ambitious, scheming, hopeful antics of the ape no longer work for us and we are left stranded in one of those peak moments that are both ecstatic and terrifying. Meaning is not something we can strive for but something that occasionally occurs during the course of a life. This makes a certain amount of sense.

So, too, does the idea that animals, lacking in the rationality and sophistication that beleaguers humans, can show us another way of being in the world. It is not so much a matter of giving animals credit for being like us as recognising that, scrape away a layer or two (or three or four) of simian social conditioning, we might find what we share.

For a time, Rowlands lived a wolf's life. He adapted his life to the needs of the wolf because Brenin was not able to adapt totally to a human routine—he could not become a dog. He could not, for example, be left alone either at home or in the car, inclined as he was to tear both apart. So everywhere Rowlands went, the wolf went, too. Some people might see this as a bit weird, but you sense that in becoming a wolf's companion Rowlands was living at a purer, more primeval, level than most of us ever access. And haven't stories of humans who live with animals, or are brought up by them, always fascinated?

Australian writer Eva Hornung in her novel *Dog Boy* dives straight into this territory. Set in Moscow during a period of turmoil and civic disintegration it concerns a very young abandoned boy who is taken in by a pack of city dogs. They exist on the margins, making a lair for themselves in an abandoned building and finding food where they can. The mother dog cares for the boy, Romochka, raises him and supervises his first excursions into the city. What is most striking about the book is how the child grows to adolescence as both a dog and a human. The other dogs are his brothers and sisters, yet all are aware that there is something non-dog about Romochka. He has vulnerabilities, and talents, that make him different, which means they must look out for him. Yet difference does not impede loyalty and mutual love. Hornung's dog family is vivid and believable, but is it possible that events could really unfold like this? Would a clan of dogs really take a child into their fold, or is that a romantic device—truly anthropomorphic in ascribing to dogs the impulses and behaviours one would sentimentally like to imagine they might feel, because it is what you would hope a human family might feel towards an abandoned child?

From Romulus and Remus—the mythological twins raised by a wolf—to Rudyard Kipling's Mowgli in *The Jungle Book* and Edgar Rice Burroughs's *Tarzan of the Apes*, these stories have such a hold on our imaginations. We long to make connections across species, and live out that desire daily with our own familiar animals. Stories such as Hornung's take us to the next mythic level, making it seem possible to be both animal and human. Yet almost always in such stories the human impulse wins—in the end the dog-child always chooses the human path if given the option. In the same way, animals turn feral, turn back to their own and make their own lives with their own kind. Except not always: cats and dogs show remarkable fidelity to their human companions. Eschewing freedom, some go to extraordinary lengths to find their way home.

Friendship between members of different species is a source of constant wonder. We are so accustomed to seeing ourselves as unique that it enthrals us when we see overt friendship and affection between an animal and a human, and even more where the friendship is between different animal species. So indoctrinated are we in the belief of our specialness that it surprises us when an animal displays emotions that have traditionally been seen as distinctly human. The devotion of dogs is legendary but what of the devotion between one particular dog and an orang-utan, or between a dog and an elephant, or a rhinoceros and a tortoise? These are true-life examples. In the first case, the orang-utan, who lived in a wildlife refuge, met up one day with a stray dog and they immediately fell into each other's arms, literally like long-lost friends. They became inseparable playmates. Posing for a photo, the blue speckled hound-dog sits regally beside his friend, the six-year-old male orang-utan. The orang-utan's arm is draped over his friend's shoulder.

Rather different in size were the elephant and her Labrador pal, who wandered around their refuge together, sat together, and just generally insisted on being together. The young male rhinoceros was lonely and a little lost when he arrived at his refuge and was put in an enclosure with a very old large tortoise. They bonded, slept together, ate together, and groomed each other.

These cases occurred in captivity and it could be argued that the experience of being in an unnatural environment affected the animals psychologically so that they behaved abnormally. Stress and loneliness pushed them into unusual alliances. Yet neither the orang-utan nor the elephant was without company of their own kind. They had plenty of that, but they each chose a dog as their mate. It is perhaps not surprising that a dog should befriend an orang-utan: like humans, just another ape. And apes, like humans, make friends. Rowlands says the kind of alliance-building that apes do, to get what they want, is unknown among wolves. But dogs may be capable of it, perhaps having learnt it from us during our long association. An alliance is more than a friendship; it means working together.

When Susan and I met, my Scruffy formed a strong alliance with her dog, Jed, a large German Shepherd. Scruffy displayed towards Jed something I have never seen in another dog: generosity. It manifested itself most spectacularly when we were living in Susan's house in Sydney. It did not take Scruffy very long to work out how to climb out of the yard. But he only did this at night and would always be home by morning. Climbing the fence was beyond Jed and he was forced to stay at home. The only way we knew about these night-time escapades was that Scruffy would always bring something home for Jed: the remains of a chicken in its foil bag or the remains of a loaf of bread. And the wrappings from these would be scattered across the front yard. Interestingly, it never occurred to Scruffy to hide the evidence—as an ape might do.

When Scruffy first met Jed, it was instant friendship. They delighted in one another; perhaps they delighted in their difference: Jed the imposing, big German Shepherd; Scruffy the cheeky little escape artist. When Jed died, Scruffy was inconsolable. A few weeks later, to try to distract him, we acquired a puppy but it took some time before Scruffy showed much interest in the puppy. Even as Jack grew, it was clear that Scruffy regarded him as a poor substitute to be condescended to, not as an equal. At best, he was a reluctant uncle to Jack.

As with humans, friendship has a lot to do with needing company. When we acquired the donkey, Lina, it was in part as a friend for two old horses we then had. We were told that donkeys were good at making friends across species and that she would get on with both horses and cows, which she did. But these days I don't think Lina is particularly close to any of the other animals, with the possible exception of the mare, Chelsea. They share a paddock so have become companions. Lina seems to regard the horses in general rather dismissively. There is a distinct air of superiority in her dealings with them, even if she is skittering out of their way (Jim in particular likes to pretend he can boss her about). She flicks her tail and tosses her head as if to say, *I don't give a shit about you.* She has sussed that in this universe it is people that matter.

As she grew older, I bought Lina a black Shetland saved from death at the sales. For all the world Dexter, as we called him, was like the Queen's Shetland: to be used for ceremonial occasions (although not as groomed), to be a companion of her own size. It did not work. For years she ignored Dexter. Eventually, as he followed her around all the time, she softened but was still very much the boss.

I know little about Lina's background. I don't think she was ever illtreated as she has always been a steady, friendly character. But over the years she has deepened her attachment to us, and to her home. I do not doubt that she loves us, as we love her. It is a two-way love that continues to grow. She shows her affection readily and knows it is returned.

Clearly animals, be they domestic or wild, recognise the individuality of one another. They may not bestow names as we do with each other and with them, but they recognise each other as separate beings. The stream of TV wildlife programs has convinced most people of that. In the wild, animals will sometimes stay with an injured friend, even to their own detriment. They seem to be able to show compassion to one another, or at least what we would call compassion. Gorillas and elephants have been tracked moving through their territory with an injured companion: the whole group regulates its pace to that of the slowest member.

One of the most renowned of all human / 'wild' animal friendships was that between Australians Anthony 'Ace' Bourke and John Rendall and the lion Christian, whom they bought as a cub from Harrods department store in December 1969. For several months, they raised Christian in their Chelsea flat above the King's Road furniture store—the aptly named Sophisticat—where they worked. The shop's customers, who included Diana Rigg and Mia Farrow, might encounter Christian stretched out on an antique pine table, or sitting regally in the shop window gazing at the exotic passing human parade along the Swinging Sixties' hippest street. Christian rode in the back of a Bentley, visited the lion statues in Trafalgar Square, exercised in a local walled churchyard and soon became a celebrity as newspapers and television stations came courting.

Christian grew up cuddlesome and playful, a big kitten. 'He was very healthy and had a beautiful nature,' Ace and John wrote in their memoir, *A Lion Called Christian*. 'He was even-tempered, and not easily alarmed or frightened. These qualities were reinforced by his trust in us and his strong feeling of security.'[20] Only once did he give them cause to be concerned when, having run off with a fur belt, he refused to relinquish it. He flattened his ears and snarled a ferocious warning. It was a reminder of his potential danger.

By the time he was eight months old and weighed nearly sixty kilos, Ace and John knew he was too large to keep in the city and they investigated a solution. They did not want Christian to go to a zoo. Eventually, they took him to Kenya to the wildlife park run by George Adamson, who, with his wife Joy, was depicted in the popular 1966 film *Born Free*.

Ace and John weren't sure if Christian, having been raised in Chelsea, would make the transition to a natural environment in Africa. But he thrived in his new lion life. The young Australians were told he would forget them. But when they returned after a year, Christian not only recognised them but greeted them joyfully. Enfolded in their arms, his big paws on their shoulders, he rubbed his face against theirs, clearly as excited and thrilled as they were. After footage emerged of this 1971 reunion between two men and a lion, it was viewed more than 16 million times on YouTube and picked up by Oprah Winfrey. Christian's bond with the men, particularly Ace Bourke, is clear to see.

A year later they went back to Kenya to see him again. He was fully grown and weighed an estimated 220 kilos. Although he didn't leap all over Ace and John this time, he still recognised them and sat with them during their time together. Afterwards, Christian went into the wild and was never seen again.

From the footage, the men's joy and love for the lion are clear. And so, too, is the lion's feelings for them. In one frame, George Adamson can be seen looking on in amazement. The lion had a very unusual upbringing but he formed an attachment that he was able to take with him into his next life. There had been another cub in the cage with Christian that day in Harrods. If the two men had decided to take that one instead, would the story have been different? Quite possibly. This was an individual love story.

*

In *When Elephants Weep*, Jeffrey Masson describes how the temporal glands of elephants stream with fluid when they are joyful. 'Elephantine joy is recognised as joy because it resembles human joy,' he wrote. 'Yet we should not assume it is identical joy. After all, we have no idea how it feels when one's temporal glands are streaming fluid. There may well be forms of joy in elephant society unrecognisable, unintelligible or simply unknown to human experience.'[21]

Charles Darwin believed that when experiencing a certain emotion—fear, for example—an animal's body responds in much the same way that a human's would under similar circumstances. But it may well be, as Masson intimates, that there are some emotional or psychological states other species have that are beyond our ken. We can sometimes recognise an emotion in an animal as being like our own but there can be other times when we get it completely wrong. For example, when a cat stops amid an altercation and begins to lick her fur it is not because she has lost interest and is calm—quite the opposite. She is cooling her raised body temperature.

Sometimes we think we know our animals better than we do. The fascination of them is largely the way in which they can be so transparent one moment and such a mystery the next.

Chapter 8
Familiarity and Difference

When I was about six years old and my sister Jenny was twelve, we got our first horse, Trooper. Trooper was Jenny's horse. She was uncertain of his breeding, but he had the look of an Australian Waler, the horses that carried thousands of soldiers into battle during World War I. Of the 160,000 of these horses that were sent overseas, only 12,000 survived.

Trooper had a shortish back, was about fourteen hands high and a taffy colour—dusty brown all over, including mane and tail. We moved to a couple of acres of land and there was a paddock for Trooper with a creek at the bottom.

It was not long after this that I got my first horse, a black mare called Beauty. We'd moved house by then, to a place that didn't have a paddock, so Beauty and Trooper lived together in a large paddock that was owned by my best friend Lea's uncle. Often on weekends, we would tether them overnight on an empty stretch of grass near where we lived, ferrying buckets of water to them. And during the day, we'd be hardly off their backs. But when we were, they were tied to our suburban fence where they would doze for hours. Beauty was a wonderful mare, kind and willing. I don't remember either of the horses ever being sick or lame. Getting them shod every six to eight weeks involved a tiring day-long ritual: riding for ninety minutes or so to the nearest blacksmith's forge, waiting around for hours while all the horses were shod—we often went with friends—then riding home again. I was probably about eight years old at this time.

Soon after, my parents bought an empty hundred acres near Cessnock, intending to move there, although in the end we only ever used it as a weekender. My father and grandfather spent whatever time they could working on the place. They built a tin shed with a wood-burning stove and a water tank, and some cattle yards, and started putting up paddock fences. In the school holidays, I spent long stretches at the farm with them. While they worked, I rode around the property on my own, bareback, and in hot weather I wore nothing but a pair of shorts.

The horses were left to their own devices for long stretches when we were tied to our city life. And there was a period when Beauty refused to be caught. I realise now that her life had changed dramatically, from being constantly handled and cosseted to virtually the open range. Was she freaked out by the change, feeling abandoned, or was she revelling in the freedom? Possibly a little of both.

We did not, in the end, move permanently to the farm. We moved to the edges of the city, to an old house on several acres, the place where Elsie the goat entered the story. While Elsie ate the lantana and Dad put up more fences, I befriended some of the local kids and taught them to ride, on Beauty and another mare we had acquired, Gypsy.

These few acres on the fringes of the city were like a mini-farm. Dad had brought a couple of the cows with us, which he milked by hand; there were the horses, and there was Elsie. The horses were not locked up at night but were fed the usual chaff and bran, their feed tins spread a little apart from one another. I remember the utter contentment of leaning on the paddock gate at dusk, listening to them munching, while the milking cow grazed off to one side in the paddock of kikuyu that was kept for her. And Elsie bleated her last calls before dark.

It was some years later that we began regularly stabling our horses when riding turned from an interest into something more, after Jenny acquired another one: Lochinvar, a beautiful thoroughbred show horse. It must have been the experience of having Lochinvar—the impact that a wonderful horse can have—that made Jenny decide to turn riding from an interest into a career.

A couple of years later we were all on our way to England and after a few months of doing the Aussies-on-the-road campervan tour of Europe, Jenny and I went to train at a riding school on the edge of London. I was only fourteen and had been allowed a year off school for the big adventure. At the riding school we were 'working pupils' and I have never worked so hard in my life: an endless round of mucking out of stables and carting buckets of water which, when you spilt any, turned instantly to ice on the cold concrete of the stable yard. It was a bitter winter. I was constantly ravenous. I'm not sure I learnt much, apart from how to muck out a stable well.

When we came back from England we moved again, this time so Jenny could open her riding school. The riding school was a family business: Mum mucked out stables in the morning before going off to her art gallery; I gave lessons on weekends, although I was an appalling teacher. I remember two pupils in particular, a girl about ten and her brother, who was maybe eight. I was sixteen or seventeen by then. They were not natural riders but that hardly excuses the way I screamed at them. They came every Saturday and their father would sit placidly on the sidelines watching, apparently unconcerned at my 'teaching method', or lack of. They kept returning week after week! I wished they wouldn't. I think Jenny eventually took over their lessons.

Beauty and Gypsy are long gone and, like Elsie, I have no idea what became of them. That astounds me now. How is it possible that I do not recall the fate of my first horse? I do not even know for sure if one or both were sold or if one of them died. It is possible, I suppose, that I may have been so traumatised by either fate for Beauty that I have completely blocked it. Then there was a big break—years—when I didn't ride.

*

I had a dream the other night that reflected my current preoccupation with animals, their behaviour and feelings. I was walking through a lush green park or meadow that was full of people picnicking and children playing, and animals were everywhere, and they were a part of what was going on. None of the animals was fighting or getting excited—they were simply *there*. There were horses and cows and dogs, and probably other animals as well. At one point, people and animals were strolling along together—a beautiful horse that looked as if it had just stepped out of the show ring moved through the green field ahead of us, its head high, observing all around it. People sat under umbrellas or on picnic rugs while their animals fed nearby, none of them tied up or on a lead. It was peaceable, companionable and beautiful, as if it were perfectly normal for people to take their horses and cows as well as their dogs when they went for a picnic.

I've been wondering lately to what extent we can befriend these larger animals. How socialised can they become? Even with our three horses and a donkey, we've found that they enjoy the rituals of our interaction. They *like* coming into the barn at night, even when they must know they are going to be locked up with only a little bit of dinner. Just being around us, being brushed, and being part of the conversation seems to keep them calm and happy. When you are around animals a lot, you learn their likes and dislikes. They also learn from us—learn what is expected of them. This applies to large animals like horses and cows as well as to small ones like cats and dogs. I'm not so sure about sheep.

I've often been intrigued to see how, when a group of animals live together, they develop their own rituals, their own culture of behaviour, and how this is transmitted to any newcomers to the group. The newcomer learns how they are meant to behave, *how things are done around here*, which is what acculturation is. I've seen it as getting to know the routines, and it is that, but it's more than that, too. Their mental clocks line up but so do other rhythms: pace of life, peacefulness (or lack of it) and safety. They learn the culture of the place, its mores. *Mores*—morality.

When the old gelding Jim first arrived, he was accustomed to living on his own in a paddock. To have company must have been a great contentment for him. One of his favourite things is to stand with another horse, giving each other a back scratch, running teeth and muzzles over the back, withers, sides and rump of the other horse. Jim always initiates it and the other horse always tires of it first and moves away—Jim would stand there back-scratching for hours if someone else would be into it.

Initially, we didn't lock Jim up at night—I like him to be able to move his old bones as much as possible. But lately, he has taken to standing, and even lying, in the shelter at the side of the barn, where he can be close to the others. In the mornings, Chelsea gets let out early but Vincent often has his morning feed inside. He likes to have company in the stable (*likes*—is calm, relaxed and good-tempered, as opposed to restless, anxious and distressed) so we started putting Jim in next to him while Vincent ate his feed. Jim originally didn't like being put in the stable and would walk around and around in it. Now he goes in willingly and is quite content. He gets a little bit of hay and is happy to stay there for hours. When I go up to let him out, he is quite often taking advantage of the soft bedding to have an extra nap.

These are new routines that Jim has learnt in his dotage, and which he seems to have taken to. We've now built a yard off the side of the barn shelter, so he is shut in there at night to keep him off the grass—he was getting very fat in the spring. He has enough room to move about in the night, a nice soft bed under the shelter, out of the wind and rain, and the company of other horses. He seems to be thriving. And happy.

Are there feelings that animals have that humans do not? Quite possibly. Sometimes when I am mystified by Vincent, for example, it could be that he is experiencing something that I have no knowledge of. When he is gazing over the stable door, perhaps he is admiring the light on the clouds, or meditating, or maybe there is something else going on that I have no conception of. If, as commonly believed, they are less 'rational' than us, then maybe what they feel is all the more intense.

Charles Darwin said we underestimate the richness of the mental lives of animals. *The Expression of the Emotions in Man and Animals* is detailed in its observations and anecdotes on the subject. Darwin noticed how one of his dogs, a terrier, behaved after she had lost her puppies. 'I was much struck with the manner in which she then tried to satisfy her instinctive maternal love by expending it on me; and her desire to lick my hands rose to an insatiable passion,' he noted.[22]

He wrote about the ability of animals to express themselves in a way that is similar to humans: 'I have seen a dog much terrified at a band of musicians who were playing loudly outside the house, with every muscle of his body trembling, with his heart palpitating so quickly that the beats could hardly be counted, and panting for breath with widely open mouth, in the same manner as a terrified man does. Yet this dog had not exerted himself; he had only wandered slowly and restlessly about the room, and the day was cold.'

The Australian zoologist and geneticist Charles Birch has commented: '[Darwin] wrote about non-humans...experiencing pleasure, pain, terror, suspicion, fear, jealousy, self-complacency, pride, curiosity, anxiety, grief, dejection, despair, joy, love, devotion, sulkiness, disdain, disgust, patience, surprise and astonishment...He showed his contemporaries that animals are much more like them than they cared to admit.'[23]

It is not just the behaviour but its cause, which has to be consistent for us to be convinced that animals are feeling a certain thing. Yet behaviour, cause and feeling may not line up in an animal in quite the way we are accustomed to seeing these things in ourselves. Susan has acquired a little dog, Sarah, who often behaves in a way and appears to be feeling things that I cannot make sense of. But no doubt it makes perfect sense to her. She is a very individual little dog, with responses and predilections unlike any dog I have known before.

Sarah was about ten years old when she came to live with us. Until then, she was owned by a devoted dog owner who kept many dogs. She was being dominated by the owner's new favourite, a dog even smaller than Sarah but yappy and aggressive towards her. Sarah, a Yorkshire terrier–Chihuahua–Shih Tzu mix, jumped into Susan's arms as soon as she saw her and sat on her lap, obviously eager to get away from her tiny enemy. But once installed at the farm, she never jumped into anyone's arms again. Rarely did she favour lap-sitting. Despite her good looks and silky golden hair, Sarah is not demonstrative and doesn't like being petted.

I think there are power issues. When Susan and Sarah go for a walk, Sarah appears to be in command—she leads the way.

At our holiday house in the Northern Rivers where we spend a few months each winter, Sarah behaves in ways she never does at the farm. When Susan has an afternoon nap on the farm, Sarah takes no notice. At the holiday house, she watches intently as Susan settles on a daybed in a living area. Only when Susan is falling asleep will Sarah crawl into her own bed underneath the TV, and she stays there until Susan stirs.

At the farm, Sarah never follows anyone to the toilet. Up north, she follows Susan and licks her hand. Why these new behaviours? Is it because at the holiday house Sarah can more readily see Susan napping and mirrors that behaviour? In the toilet, does she feel she has better access to her Susan than in a smaller toilet at the farm?

A mystery. But that's Sarah.

Chapter 9
Why Scientists tie Themselves into Linguistic Knots

In the past, the kinds of work undertaken by animal behaviourists often seems to have had very little to do with the real world of animals and what we might learn from them simply by observing them. For decades behavioural scientists spoke of animals having 'exploratory urges' rather than curiosity, or exhibiting an 'impulse to flee' rather than fear, or 'instinctual bonding' rather than love. Things are changing as the evidence mounts of the special talents and abilities of a great many animals, from octopi to elephants, parrots to dolphins. But that long refusal of scientists to credit animals with having emotions has had ramifications: it closed down avenues of inquiry instead of opening them up, thereby holding back our understanding. Worse, it led to thousands of experiments of downright cruelty.

In *The Philosopher and the Wolf*, Mark Rowlands describes one such experiment invented by three Harvard psychologists, which involved putting a dog in a 'shuttlebox'. The box comprised two compartments and the floor of each was an electrified grid. The experiment consisted of putting a dog in one compartment and giving an intense electric shock to the feet, so the dog would jump into the other compartment. Then there would be another electric shock so the dog jumped back, and so on. This was repeated not once or twice but hundreds of times in any one experiment, and the divider between the compartments was raised each time so it became more and more difficult for the dog to jump. The dog, initially agitated and whimpering, gradually tired. Then, in a refinement of the torture, the floor of both grids was electrified simultaneously. The dog lay there exhausted, trembling, pissing, and defecating. Destroyed.

The experimenters, and Rowlands names them—R. Solomon, K. Kamin and L. Wynne—said they were looking into the learned helplessness theory of depression. This is a psychological phenomenon whereby people who face repeated adversity lose the capacity to improve their situation, even when opportunities are available. Such experiments continued for years. Dogs were still being put in shuttleboxes in the 1960s when researcher Martin Seligman performed experiments that would have alarming ramifications.

Seligman subjected two groups of dogs to electric shocks in a shuttle-box. One group could escape—and quickly learned that if they jumped across a barrier, the shocks stopped. The other group could not stop the shocks, no matter what they did. They gave up trying to escape their torment, becoming powerless and passive.

In the wake of the 9/11 terror attacks, America's Central Intelligence Agency took a renewed interest in such experiments and in learned helplessness. The agency contracted two military psychologists, one an admirer of Seligman's work, to develop 'enhanced' techniques for interrogating Al Qaeda suspects. The psychologists believed the learned helplessness theory provided a basis for brutal techniques, including waterboarding. The idea was that detainees would become passive and depressed in response to adverse or uncontrollable events and yield information, according to a 2014 US Senate report on the CIA's torture program.[24] The report concluded that the techniques did not add valuable information to what had already been obtained through less brutal means. Seligman, today an author of popular self-help books and a former president of the American Psychological Association, was 'horrified that good science...may have been used for such bad purposes'.[25]

Dogs continue to suffer in the name of 'good' science. They have been force-fed pesticides, implanted with pacemakers, bred to have fatal diseases, and invariably killed when the research is over. In the US alone, more than 40,000 dogs were estimated to have been used in medical experiments in 2020.[26]

*

Scientists tie themselves in knots of linguistic nonsense rather than report the simplest, commonsense reasons for why animals do some of the things we observe them doing. There has been such determination to see humans as unique and special. To agree we are mammals on the one hand, but on the other insist on the chasm between us and other animals. And this at the same time as animals are being used in experiments as stand-ins for humans. One of the common myths about animals is that they are colourblind. But the difference, rather, is that while apes like us are trichromats, other mammals like cats and dogs are dichromats, which means they have a smaller range of vision. So there is no reason, for example, why an ape might not have just the same sort of fascination with the splendour of a setting sun as a human. Indeed, a wild chimpanzee has been observed gazing at a particularly beautiful sunset for a quarter of an hour, until it was dark, Jeffrey Masson, the author of several books on the emotional lives of animals, noted in *When Elephants Weep*.

'If animals were without colour vision, of what benefit would be a baboon's brightly coloured face and rump, or a peacock's tail?' Masson asks.[27] Or, indeed, why would a male bowerbird choose only pieces of a particular blue with which to decorate his bower? A female might visit the bowers of several males before deciding to mate. 'The male does not decide to decorate with blue objects because, let us say, they are rare, or because he knows that will indicate to females that he ranges over a wide area due to his good genes. It is more parsimonious to postulate that both female and male bowerbirds like the way the blue looks,' Masson argues. In choosing her mate based on the beauty of his bower, a female bowerbird is showing an aesthetic sensibility. Perhaps one not so very different from our own.

75

Certainly Darwin was convinced that, as with humans, some animals possessed a refined aesthetic sense: 'It can hardly be doubted that many animals are capable of appreciating beautiful colours and even forms, as is shown by the pains which the individuals of one sex take in displaying their beauty before those of the opposite sex.'[28] So, too, with the sense of taste. Most animals enjoy sweet foods and dislike bitter ones. To disguise medicine in feed, we often add molasses to a horse's dinner.

If animals have a sense of individuality, affection, beauty and pleasure, are they self-conscious? Is all mental activity in animals unconscious, the way much of human thinking is unconscious, or are they consciously aware of their thoughts? The adaptability of behaviour in changing circumstances suggests conscious behaviour.

We see another example of this repeatedly: Jan looks after our animals when we go away and the dogs, in particular, slip immediately into a new routine when they are with her—they adapt their behaviour to her ways. Within minutes of our departure, their despair at our disappearance fades and they know they will now follow Jan's rules and routines. This is different from ours, but so strong in the dogs' memories that they quickly switch to it. Humans might well envy their ready adaptability.

But are they aware of themselves as conscious beings? It has usually been thought not. It has been assumed that they are not rational and therefore do not have the kind of thought processes that would allow them to reflect on their behaviour. But what does 'reflect' mean? It may well be true that they cannot think back, as we can, on events of months or years before. But they can certainly recognise familiar situations and the way they react to that situation will be a direct result of that earlier experience.

Masson gives the example of a mountain goat who sees a predator. It will often walk away calmly and slowly until it is out of sight. Then it will immediately bolt. This is a kind of subterfuge. But is it thought through? Is it 'instinctual'? Is it the result of an earlier experience, an accidental discovery? Masson believes such an action shows an animal acting as if conscious that others are perceiving its behaviour.

If a bird goes to a particular location for food, the simplest explanation is that it knew there was a good source of food so remembered the route and went there—rather than getting caught up in elaborate webs of stimulus and response, as behaviourists have been inclined to do.

It is now known that there are complex forms of communication between members of certain species. For example, honey bees make complex dances to impart information to one another regarding a good source of food. In groundbreaking work, German ethologist Karl von Frisch identified two distinct dances. The round dance tells of the location of a particularly rich source of food quite close to the hive, maybe less than 100 metres. It doesn't tell direction, just that the food is within that 100 metres. The second dance is the waggle dance and is used to describe sources of food that are more distant. It involves circles, straight lines and a wagging motion. The longer it takes to perform one circuit of the dance, the further away the source of food. Von Frisch even worked out how far: if the dance only lasts a second and a half, the food is within 300 metres. If it takes five seconds, it is a couple of kilometres away.

Apiarists, scientists and other observers had pondered the ability of bees to communicate with each other long before von Frisch. Even Aristotle had observed the insects' curious movements. But von Frisch, who was awarded the Nobel Prize for his work in 1973, was the first to figure out what was going on. His decoding of the complexity of bee communication transformed how we understand another species.

'While all animals communicate, the means they use and the subjects about which they communicate can vary from species to species. These separate systems of communication might be said to be languages of the animal kingdom,' nature writer Bil Gilbert noted.[29] Vervet monkeys, for example, give quite different alarm calls depending on the threat: if a leopard is about, the signal alerts the others to run into trees. For eagles, it makes them look up into the air and run into bushes. For snakes, the call makes them stand on their hind legs and look into the grass.

Several reasons suggest animals have consciousness. For example, their behaviour is similar to ours, which we know is conscious for us. Their physiology and biochemistry are similar to ours; adaptable behaviour is explained more simply and directly by assuming it is conscious, and complex means of communication between animals suggest consciousness.

Often when their behaviour is like ours—when they are startled, for example—we would react in the same way *instinctively*. So I'm not sure if that is proof that they are conscious. But nor is it proof of the reverse. Certainly many species show signs that suggest they have feelings and emotions, and that those feelings and emotions matter to them.

One sign of self-consciousness is the way that some animals hate being laughed at. They somehow know what such laughter means. I'm thinking of dogs now. They can tell the difference between joyful laughter—people being happy, which they love and sometimes try to join in on by yelping or leaping—and derisory laughter. Masson suggests that dogs don't laugh among themselves but maybe when they are playing together and grin in that happy way, maybe that *feels* like laughter.

When a dog is ashamed of something it has done it shows this clearly, skulking about or creeping up and licking your hand pleadingly, asking for forgiveness. 'Ritual submission', the scientist would call it, which describes the action but it doesn't describe what the dog is feeling. Perhaps it is acting out an emotion that we might feel but in similar circumstances try to hide: shame.

I have another example of conscious behaviour from when, as a teenager, I took to riding Jenny's slightly crazy mare Suzy Q. Among other odd behaviours, she was adept at feigning lameness. Out in the paddock, there would be no sign that she was sore. She'd trot and canter and spin about and be perfectly fine. But catch her and saddle her up and she would immediately appear lame. We thought it was perhaps intermittent lameness but I always suspected that she was putting it on to get back to her own pursuits.

Chapter 10
Communication

When I was introduced to the work of European horse trainer Klaus Hempfling I was sceptical. Hempfling specialises in human–horse communication and movement. What he can do with a horse without a bridle, without even a lead around its neck, is interesting. But he works mainly on the ground—what did this have to do with riding?

He does ride but when he does, it is mostly without a bridle. He looks pretty ordinary on the horse—more scepticism on my part. Because, as with most horse people, I've always been intent on the riding: on what the rider does, on the accomplishment of riding, the discipline, and the training of the horse to do what we want while on its back.

I have to admit that the way Hempfling can communicate with a horse and turn it from a combative or standoffish animal into a cooperative one is pretty impressive. He communicates with horses through his body language. He believes that every movement by a horse or human conveys information. A misplaced movement or misunderstood gesture can mean the difference between success or failure in the relationship with a horse. So attuned can he and the horse become to one another that they can literally dance together, the horse mirroring the trainer's steps. But part of me still says, *But this is for people who can't ride or who have become frustrated with their riding ability and given up.* And after thinking this I realise that for me riding has been something that *I do*. It has only peripherally been about establishing a real relationship with the horse. I stand in the barn and look at Vincent in a new way.

*

For American horse trainer Carolyn Resnick, the 'being with' is where it all begins. She came to understand horses after spending childhood summers hanging out with a mob of wild mustangs. She believes that if you are to have a good relationship, a horse must accept you into its world, and this means observing their habits and routines, rituals and instincts. She ended up being able to ride the lead mustang mare without a saddle or bridle after, she believes, being accepted as part of the herd. Her method, part of a strand of thinking known as 'natural horsemanship', emphasises the essential liberty of the horse and believes that a horse can and will choose to be with a human and to do what that human wishes. She takes this thinking right through from wild horses to advanced dressage horses.

At the other end of the spectrum is Andrew McLean, the prime exponent of learning theory in Australian horse circles. He also works with dressage horses. To him, training a horse is not about trust or trying to get on the same wavelength as the horse. It is about consistency and kindness; a strict regime of asking for a response and rewarding when it is given.

It is often said of a horse that he or she 'enjoys their work' or is 'willing'. Riding horses, particularly those trained as competition horses, can often partake enthusiastically in the task they are given, be that jumping, galloping or performing a string of flying changes in the dressage arena. They have a job and know how to do it and so enjoy it. They have *funktionlust*. A purpose, a role in life, a partnership perhaps with a person they have bonded with. It is all too evident when a horse does not have that, when they are unwilling.

Ultimately a horse is a very large animal that cannot really be forced to do anything. They can, however, be coerced into passivity, into a form of learned helplessness. Some horses thrive on a certain type of work; another horse may find the same tasks overwhelming, and become stressed, depressed and ill. Issues around the welfare of performance horses are going to become more controversial as the general public becomes more interested in animal welfare. The real issue, for the many owners and trainers who do treat their animals well, is understanding the ability and individuality of each animal and assessing its suitability for the task being asked of it.

Adherents of learning theory appear to believe that all horses are the same; press the same buttons and you will get the same response. This denies the individuality of the animal, their special strengths and their unique personalities.

*

In the spirit of learning about my animals by consciously observing them, I've been spending time just being with the horses. The other day I sat down on a bank in one of the horse paddocks. Chelsea was grazing nearby; Lina a good way off. When Chelsea realised that I was just sitting there, in the middle of their paddock, not something I would normally do, she raised her head high, pricked her ears and began walking towards me. Then she stopped and watched me. Suddenly she trotted to one side, stopped, and then approached again, blowing through her nose. Then stopped and watched again.

Vincent and old Jim, in the adjacent paddock, became aware that something odd was happening. They stopped grazing and stared. Then they began to approach. Then stopped and stared again. All three were now quite close, and watching me.

Lina, a long way off up the gully, realised something was afoot and began to approach at a steady and deliberate walk. Chelsea then came right up to me and sniffed my foot. Vinnie was just on the other side of the fence, looking very interested. Jim came up and pushed Vinnie out of the way. Chelsea sniffed my knee and my hand and notebook.

What is she up to? I could hear them thinking. Lina stopped a little distance away, apparently not interested in coming nearer.

I lay back on the grass and put my hat over my face. Chelsea nuzzled my shoe, then ate some grass next to it. Jim and Vincent stood under a tree and began nuzzling each other's withers, the old you-scratch-my-back-and-I'll-scratch-yours. But Vinnie couldn't be bothered.

Chelsea began to lose interest and started chewing on some bark. It was as if I had visited their world and they were not quite sure what to make of it, what it meant, or what to do about it. Chelsea blew through her nose in a relaxed way and wandered off. Lina and Jim resumed grazing. After about half an hour they all wandered off, Lina the last to go. But Vincent stayed closest.

Then a big kangaroo hopped down the hill on the neighbour's side of the fence. Jim was very interested in it but Vincent was not much at all—he grew up near Canberra and probably saw kangaroos all the time when he was young.

Later in the day, when I went out to bring them in just before a big storm hit, Jim and Vincent were behaving strangely—well, like a pair of stallions, really. They were running in circles around each other, pawing the ground, rearing. Vincent gave a couple of enormous bucks and cantered along beside the fence. Chelsea was on the other side. Then he stopped and started pawing again, as if about to roll but I don't think that was it. Then Jim raced up and started circling him and pawing.

I worked it out: they were strutting their stuff in front of Chelsea, each trying to keep the other away from her. A couple of times Jim tried to bite Vincent. Although they are both geldings they were trying to compete for Chelsea's attention. She is probably in season.

*

I've been observing the different affection/rejection habits of the cat and the horse. It is not unusual to find a degree of sympathy between a cat and a horse and, strangely, I have found in the past certain similarities in the personalities of my cats and horses. Vincent is quite fond of cats.

Within days of the cat Charlie arriving, it was clear that he preferred indoors to out. He likes to sit on the armchair in my study and watch the birds on the other side of the glass window. He peers intently and thumps his tail on the upholstery. Then when they move off he settles down to snooze again.

It is as if, during his time as a stray, he had more adventures than he ever wants to have again. He is scared of our old dog Jackie and nervous about sharp noises. He snarls and hisses ferociously if he sees Jackie outside; inside the house he has been more prepared to tolerate her. Then yesterday he approached her and me in the kitchen. Jackie was lying down near the back door and I was standing next to her. I don't know whether Charlie wanted to go out the door or whether he thought Jack might get some of his food that was out on the porch, but he began to approach and started snarling as he did so. My legs were in between him and poor old Jackie, which was a little worrying. I reached for the door and opened it so Charlie could go out if that was what he wanted. But he stood still about a metre or so from us and just kept on snarling. I motioned to him to go out and he hissed and spat at me. I slapped him and he scuttled away to the other end of the house. He didn't come out for a while and was a little subdued when he did.

What was he trying to do at that time? Leave? Attack Jack? Very odd.

These are his only instances of misbehaving. The rest of the time he is affectionate and sociable. I wonder what sort of relationship we will forge? After a lifetime of having animals, it is automatic to fall into the kind of relationship one has always had. Fond but somewhat formal with the cats—lots of stroking and sometimes even a bit of rough play, but on the whole respectful. With the dogs, a mixture of sternness and devotion—some tough love sometimes. Laying down the law—one has to do that with all of them. But with the dogs, it is a case of mutual dependence—and their eyes follow you.

Having grown up with so many different kinds of animals, I am a bit offhand with them. By looking at my relationships with them, I will become less so. Yet part of me doesn't want those relationships to be too premeditated, to lose that looseness and spontaneity.

*

It is hard to know how much of Charlie's behaviour with the dog is fear and how much is aggression. On one occasion he was lying on the bedroom carpet and suddenly leapt on my bare leg, sinking his teeth and claws in. He got a major whack for that and ran off into the hallway, where he sat licking himself to cool his body temperature. After a few minutes, I went up to him and he rubbed his head against my hand and purred, as if to say, *Okay, I deserved that.*

Vincent, too, has mysterious affection/rejection habits: I worked old Jim this morning because he is putting on too much weight. Vincent stood at his stable door watching us. After I'd finished with Jim and put him out, I went to get Vincent and he quite deliberately turned his back on me. Not in a bad-tempered way; he was just clearly and deliberately ignoring me. *What do I do with this?* I wondered. *Should I slap him on the bum?* That would have made him bad-tempered and wouldn't make him turn around. I stood at his door for a few moments in silence. Then decided to turn my back on him. I leaned my back against the door and said nothing. Within five seconds I heard him move. I kept my back turned and a few seconds later he was breathing in my ear. Then I turned around and scratched him between the eyes and said, 'Hello!' Two can play that game, Vincent.

It was a glorious cool morning and I decided to take him out for a ride in the big paddock across the gully. We were trotting briskly along when a large black bird flew up from the long grass right under Vincent's nose. It frightened him and he shied while I was rising out of the saddle. I felt myself starting to part company but thought, *Oh, I'll be all right*. Then I realised there was no way I could get back into that saddle! I was beyond the point of no return. Then I'm thinking, *Hope I don't break anything*. What I mainly felt was surprise—I haven't fallen off a horse in years!

It wasn't a heavy fall as the grass was thick, but it was a relief to hit the ground and realise I was still in one piece. Of course, I hadn't held onto the reins, as you are meant to. And I had visions of Vincent galloping for home and getting his legs caught in the reins.

But he didn't do that, just ran around me in a big circle. I think he got a bigger shock than I did. I stood up and he stopped and turned towards me. I sat back down on the ground again and rubbed my leg. He came towards me. Not right up to me, but close enough so I could stand and catch him.

I found a bank to stand on so I could get on. When we got home Vincent was still a little trembly, as though he'd frightened himself, or was frightened about getting into trouble.

*

Last night there was a television program on a man who has spent fifteen years observing a family of elephants. They became so accustomed to him that the matriarch elephant was happy to give birth in his presence, out in the open, which they don't normally do, and the young elephants treated him like a relative, coming up to greet him each morning. They knew his voice and his scent, and knew they could trust him. He felt that he had been allowed to become part of the family.

Why do we limit our relationships with animals? Or believe it is only with cats and dogs that we can have close relationships? I am sure I am not at all unusual in finding relationships with animals a lot easier than those with people. They are not laden with the same expectations.

Indeed, a relationship with an animal that is full of trust but devoid of expectation is a joyous thing. It is when expectation comes into it that things can go awry. And it seems to happen particularly with horses.

Some horses can't handle the pressure of our expectations. Why is Vincent so good one day, so bad the next? He responds to my moods—to my tiredness and tension, my *intention*. My simply being with him, and working quietly and joyfully, is his favourite way of being. The tension in his muscles after a bad workout; their softness when he has worked in a relaxed fashion. Do they mirror my muscles? If I slow down, calm and centre myself, then Vincent will, too. The very fact that he is so attuned to me, that we are so attuned to one another, means that I can, if I wish, learn a great deal from him. He will—is—showing me my shortcomings.

*

The young bull, Bill, has been put in with the cows for the first time. Bill is two years old and just in the last month or two he has begun to look like a real bull, heavily muscled and slow moving. I have decided to move him in with the cows. Susan says it is too early. He is barely a teenager. We'll see.

He did move towards the cows very slowly today, reluctant to leave his mates, the steers. He is neither afraid of humans nor aggressive towards them. He is a friendly chap in his reserved way.

When he was put in with the cows they came running towards him, some of the calves racing in front. That got the cows worried and they were keen to push Bill away from the youngsters. Bill looked a bit confused but he behaved like a gentleman as the cows pushed and shoved him. One of the first to rush up to him was young Bert, all agog at such a big bloke being in the paddock with them. Bert came to a sliding halt a metre or so from Bill and the look on his face said it all: *Wow!! You're so big!*

The cows were jostling about, the younger calves getting jammed into the corner. Then after a bit, they all calmed down and Bill decided to have a bit of a sniff. He rubbed his chin across the top of one cow's head, then turned his lips back to show his gums. Mmmm, you smell good. The cow gave him a sniff, too.

Bill's mother, Freckle, her calf and the six-month-old heifer Peggy Sue were in the next paddock so as not to get with the bull. Freckle looked at me in her gentle way, as if asking, *Why am I here on my own with just these two youngsters?* She's confused and upset about it and doesn't understand.

Bill has now been with the cows twenty-four hours and it may be that he is not up to what is required of him. I went up to the top paddock to see how he was getting on. It's a glorious early summer day. A cool breeze, green grass, fat cows.

Bill was hanging out with one cow, just following her about. He jumped up on her, pretty half-heartedly, I thought. One of the other cows then came over and obligingly showed him how it was done. Then Bill pushed her away and had another go himself, but the first cow decided to move off. A few minutes later she made it very clear that she was ready now, holding her tail up and at an odd angle, and her back humped, as if braced ready to take his weight. But Bill just sniffed her. Then the cow's bull calf, who is all of three months old, decided he could show Bill how it was done, by jumping up on Bill himself. Some cows and calves jump each other but often they end up getting the wrong end or approach from the side, not the back. But this young calf had perfect technique, he just wasn't tall enough to stay there for long—and he was jumping Bill.

Bill turned around and chased him off. The calf was not to be deterred. He kept following Bill and jumping on him if he had a chance. The cow meanwhile was loitering about with her tail cocked and her back humped. Bill had one or two attempts to mount her but seemed more concerned about the calf that kept tailing him. They wandered along the fence line, the three of them. Cow in front, then Bill, then the bull calf. This went on for half an hour or more. I began to feel quite sorry for Bill. He looked a bit harassed.

But it is only a day into Bill's adulthood and he is a bit like a teenager that tries more than he is ready for. Perhaps Susan was right: maybe he's just not old enough yet, despite his grown-up looks.

Chapter 11
Do Animals Have Souls?

There are some animals to whom we are very ready to concede souls: ourselves, of course, and other apes, dogs, perhaps horses and other creatures with grandeur and individuality. Certainly our donkey Lina has a soul, of that I have no doubt. Cows often look rather soulful, and I am easily persuaded that they might have souls. But does a sheep have a soul? We tend to think of a hierarchy of animals, and sheep do not figure high on that hierarchy. Individuality seems to be key. And sheep have the misfortune to look very like one another.

Observing a paddock full of sheep, following one another in single file like…well, sheep. Or running about in a phalanx, swerving and curving as if of one mind, it is easy to think of the flock as the unit. It is no accident that 'sheep' is both singular and plural.

But on a smallholding, where a hobby farmer may have a cow and a couple of goats and a sheep, the individuality of the sheep is immediately apparent. She is herself. And no doubt her owner will attest that she has a personality; in fact, each of the animals is an individual.

Turn again to the paddock and its flock of sheep. And see this time a large group of individuals who behave differently when alone to when they are together. When in the flock they are in sync with one another, organised and secure. Alone, they are forced into another way of being, but they can adapt to this and can be solo creatures. In this they are not so different from us.

Looking for the soul in an animal is no more difficult than looking for it in ourselves, and no easier. It is linked to the idea of the sublime. And it is there in the light of an animal's eye if we care to look. When the lights go out, for animal or human—when the eyes that expressed so much are suddenly lifeless—it is much the same for all of us. Soulful eyes one moment; empty ones the next.

Animals struggle against death, against the threat of it. Fear, flight, fight: these are responses to the risk of annihilation. So they know about the threat of death. But what does death mean to them? To us, it means the loss of any future time we may have had. We see time's arrow disappearing over the horizon and want to follow it, and death prevents that. It may mean that to animals, too, or perhaps it means something entirely different, something that we can have no conception of. It may be that life is circular, rather than linear, to them. And the threat of slaughter disrupts that sense of completion.

Death is often at one's elbow on a farm, and often I find myself hovering on that uneasy terrain between hard-headedness and sentimentality.

*

The cows and calves were gathered in a companionable group near the water trough this morning. One of them had somehow procured a branch from the pine trees across the fence and was enjoying chewing on the sap and fresh pine needles. I took it off her, concerned about what it might do to her milk. She glared, reluctant to give it up.

Susan and I stood about with them for a while, admiring the calves. There is only one purebred heifer calf—the rest are boys—and we decided to give her a name; she may remain as one of the herd. We tried a few names out and settled on Lily, in memory of the calf my father hand-raised. She is a very pretty calf, with a golden tinge to her red Hereford coat.

It is wonderful when the calves are born but not so wonderful a year or two later when we have to wave them goodbye. Of this season's calves only two of the seven are heifers. This means that there will be five more steers to send off to the slaughterhouse in a year or so.

As we were standing there, I looked over the fence to where the three big steers were grazing.

'We'll have to sell the steers soon,' I said.

'Can't they just stay and eat the grass?' Susan asked. For her, the cattle are mainly decorative.

'We'll run out of grass if we keep them all,' I said, ever the pragmatist.

This discussion happens every time we have to send cattle to market. This time, as well as the two who we call 'the twins' because they look so similar, we will be sending Plucky. Plucky arrived the day we bought our cows. He was so young we wondered if he had been born at the saleyards. The poor little thing tottered about unsteadily, pathetically bawling.

His mother wanted nothing to do with him. We even wondered whether the wrong calf had been sent with her, so determinedly did she reject him. We'd give her hay so she would stand still and let the poor little fellow near her, then we'd stand over her with a big stick and make threatening noises if she tried to kick him away. He'd get a little bit of milk that way, but he needed extra handfeeding—two or three times a day from the bucket and plastic teat. Somehow he survived, just. So we called him Plucky. He had various things wrong with him, in addition to the cranky mother. He received several courses of injections—antibiotics and vitamins. He was also a bit thick and had one wonky leg. It may be that the cow was rejecting him because she thought he'd need too much looking after.

But we humans persevered. For six weeks it was a three-times-a-day routine for Jan and me. Still Plucky wasn't thriving, and we were exhausted from the whole exercise. We decided to put cow and calf out with the rest of the herd and let nature take its course. I thought it would be the end of Plucky but there was no more we could do. All our human interference had only resulted in a sickly calf that the cow still didn't want. For a day and a half Plucky trailed the herd, often getting left behind. We'd find him curled up asleep in a gully by himself, the rest of the herd out of sight. Then, on the second evening, we saw him drinking from his mother. And she was letting him! From then on she accepted him and he made steady progress.

Unlike the other steers, Plucky has been allowed to live on at the farm into maturity. And he is now a big, beefy and very stroppy fellow with no sign of the gammy leg. But he can't abide humans—all that handling early in his life has turned him right off us. We thought we'd keep him as a kind of pet but he's not interested in being a pet. The other day he chased me, so his end is nigh.

*

When you have the power of life and death over an animal, when—as so often with one's dogs—you have to make that decision, how do you judge the end? The crossover moment between aliveness and the dwindling of life's force? We have been talking for years about Jackie's imminent demise. Her arthritis has been so bad for so long that she has lasted probably four years longer than I expected. I remember when we took her north just over four years ago. She was so tired by the journey that when we arrived, and for some days afterwards, I fully expected her not to last the winter.

As a Kelpie / German Shepherd cross, she inherited the notorious hip dysplasia so common in German Shepherds. There have been many times when her hind legs and hips would just not do what she wanted. Many times we thought she was literally on her last legs. But each time she has rallied. Her grinning mouth and shining eyes always said, *I'm still alive and still enjoying life.* Occasionally she's been through a bad patch of a day or two when her eyes have looked tired and we can tell she is in pain. Then miraculously she would recover.

She has been getting steadily slower and less able to get around. We have kept adjusting to her growing incapacity. When her hind legs first started to go, we got a ramp so she could still get in the back of the ute. That was years ago. About twelve months ago she ceased being able to climb the ramp so she was no longer able to go in 'her' ute. So we started taking her in the car once or twice a week, for a treat. She just managed to fit on the floor of the front passenger side, and she just managed to get herself in and out, with a bit of help. (If more than one human was going, the one who wasn't driving had to sit in the back, while Jackie rode in state in the front.)

She has always come inside for an hour or two after dinner, and this was a ritual she was not prepared to give up. She would rest for a while on a special mat just inside the kitchen door. Have a long drink of water while sitting there, then gradually make her way across the treacherous, slippery kitchen floor to the safety of the lounge-room carpet. She'd be happy there for another hour. But she found it increasingly hard to get up and go outside and was particularly reluctant to cross back over that treacherous kitchen floor. So the next modification was that at night, when she was going to bed, she left by the front door.

We never considered letting her stay inside overnight. Apart from concerns about her bladder, we had found when Scruffy was old that changing their routine late in life does not do them any favours. So Jackie would be helped to the front door, then given five or ten minutes to make her way towards the laundry, then one of us would go outside to supervise the final struggle up the slope to the laundry door. She'd flop onto her bed gratefully and be covered with a blanket.

Yesterday morning, I found her in the orchard, lying awkwardly on the dewy grass and unable to get up. I half carried her back to the laundry. She spent the day there, barely moving. But after dinner she seemed to want to come down to the house, so I encouraged her. Much to our surprise, she even made it across the kitchen floor to the lounge room. She lay on her special piece of carpet and grinned at us, with what looked like triumph in her eyes. But the struggle up to the laundry at bedtime was slow. I supported her under her belly, virtually carrying her back legs.

This morning, for the first time, she was not much interested in her biscuit. She cannot stand on her own. Usually, once I've helped her get to her feet, she has managed to totter about. But not now. Her left hind leg won't hold her up at all. When I manipulate it I can hear the joints moving ineffectually, like bits of Meccano that won't fit together, just jangling against each other beneath the flesh.

I brought her day mat outside and sat her on it in the fresh air. When I went down to the house I could see her sitting there, looking a bit brighter, watching the house.

Perhaps today, or tomorrow, we will have to make the decision. Declining the biscuit this morning reads to me like a sign from her. Perhaps she is finally saying, *I've had it. It's too hard.* It *is* too hard. She has been such a brave, brave girl for such a long, long time. She has withstood pain that would have felled most animals, has been stoic and found what enjoyment she could in life: food, a ride in the car, a cuddle. She should go out with her heart still strong.

*

The decision was made and Ken the vet arranged to come on Friday afternoon. Susan was reconciled to the decision; that it couldn't be put off any longer. Jackie was brought out to lie in the sun, weak as it is at this time of year, and Susan brushed her. Jackie enjoyed it so, stretching out her poor old body and rolling over so her tummy was exposed, making little moans of pleasure. She always found being brushed a bit like some people find tickling: delicious and agonising at once. For the rest of the day she lay on her bed in the laundry and worked on a large lamb bone. She had completely demolished it by the time the vet arrived. He was impressed.

Then the preparations were made. I held her shoulders and the nurse held her leg while Ken shaved it. We gave her a last stroke, then the needle with its fat syringe of thick blue liquid was inserted. She winced, then drooped and was gone even before the syringe was empty. We carried her on her blanket to the orchard. The hole had already been dug.

So another passes, another name to add to the long list of companions. And Jacko's soul? Of what did it consist and where is it now? What was it that went when the light went from her eyes? People live on in what we remember of them, and so it is with our animals—her smile, her loyalty, her joy in small pleasures. The feel of her coat and the firm narrowness of her muzzle, just above her nose. Her silliness when she was young and the calm pleasure of her company when she became older.

*

We have come north, to a relaxed little town where people are everywhere accompanied by dogs. On the streets, on the beach, under the tables at outdoor cafes, waiting outside shops. These dogs belong to their human's pack. Not children, but not 'mere pets' either. Humans and dogs give each other enjoyment and consideration—you can see it in the way they look at one another. We have one friend here who has a lively little lapdog. When Valerie has to work, she arranges for Minnie to go to a friend's house where there are dogs. Minnie spends the day playing and comes home happy and exhausted. Taking her to 'play group' and collecting her are part of Valerie's routine, as is the morning ritual of a walk on the beach with other dogs and their people. Providing all this is part of the deal that Valerie strikes for the pleasure of having this affectionate creature in her life. It is a deal that benefits them both.

*

Whenever one of my animals has died, the others of their species have shown little interest in them, in their physical remains. They don't react at all. Elephants are different; elephants are known to stand around and mourn at the side of a dead companion. But my cats and dogs and horses have never done this. The actual body appears to have little significance for them. And yet in the days and weeks that follow, they do miss their old friend. They are aware of the absence. Dogs mope and look perplexed. Horses can be agitated and distressed. Some years ago my old grey gelding died. His half-brother, with whom he had lived most of his life, got by okay—he had Lina and another horse for company—but a year or so later, when I acquired Vincent, also a grey gelding, you should have seen the response! The old boy whinnied and raced across the paddock towards Vinnie. He clearly thought it was his brother returned. When he came close and realised his mistake, he lost interest.

Chapter 12
Animal Rights—and Wrongs

The American philosopher Tom Regan, who wrote on animal rights for more than half a century, believed that the best way to think of animals is that they are 'subjects of a life'.

Some people say that animals don't have an awareness of being in the world, and that they don't know they are going to die. That they don't have souls, that they don't have language, that they don't have rational thought. All these things are put forth as reasons why animals don't have 'rights'.

Regan argued: 'The question of who has inherent value is...resolved more rationally without the introduction of the idea of immortal souls than by its use...What could be the basis of our having more inherent value than animals? Their lack of reason, or autonomy, or intellect? Only if we are willing to make the same judgement in the case of humans who are similarly deficient.'

In being 'subjects of a life' he meant that their life matters to them, that they are aware of what happens to them and have an interest in being alive. And that is the reason they have rights that should be respected. As he and others have pointed out, very young children don't necessarily have awareness of being in the world, or of death, but they still have rights.

And how does it bear on rights that animals may not have souls?

The writer, scholar and committed Christian C.S. Lewis believed that if animals didn't have souls, and therefore did not have access to eternal life, then it was even more imperative that we do not do anything to damage them in this, their only life. The absence of a soul made the infliction of pain harder to justify. 'For it means that animals cannot deserve pain, nor profit morally by the discipline of pain, nor be recompensed by happiness in another life for suffering in this,' he wrote in his 1947 essay 'Vivisection'.

Lewis was an outspoken critic of vivisection and had a deep love for animals. This passion infused all his writing, from scholarly to popular. He is best known today for his series of children's novels The Chronicles of Narnia. The seven fantasy novels are replete with talking, intelligent, noble animals and, in the case of his celebrated *The Lion, the Witch and the Wardrobe*, a mystical lion, Aslan, who is the epitome of goodness.

Although Lewis considered humans absolutely separate from animals, and on a higher level—much as he saw angels on a higher plane than humans—he believed animals had consciousness and could feel pain. 'At some point...sentience almost certainly comes in, for the higher animals have nervous systems very like our own,' he wrote in *The Problem of Pain*. Controversially, he wrote that the same arguments that favoured experimentation on animals could be used to justify experiments on humans, and made a comparison with Nazi practices. 'The Christian defender is very apt to say that we are entitled to do anything we please to animals because they "have no souls". But what does this mean? If it means that animals have no consciousness, then how is that known? They certainly behave as if they had, or at least the higher animals do.'[30]

Among Christians, there has always been an argument about the nature of animals and what we owe them. Scholars have scoured the Bible for God's direction on how we should behave towards other creatures. St Augustine, Thomas Aquinas, John Calvin and many others, right through to the present, have put forth their interpretation. The question of the soul, and whether animals have one is, for Christians, central to their thinking on this issue. For them it is a moral question, of whether God intended animals for human use or whether they are living creatures on a par with us. The Bible is not clear on this: both sides can argue a case by making direct reference to different sections within the scriptures. Calvin was inclined to believe that we were not originally meant to eat animals, that 'men were content with herbs and fruits until the deluge'.[31] After the deluge, according to Calvin, everything was altered and man had to resort to eating flesh.

Tom Regan goes further, arguing that animal flesh was not on the menu in Eden. For Regan, a philosopher, not a theologian, the unmistakable message of the creation story of Genesis is that God did not create animals for the use of, or food for, humans.

'The food we are given by God is not the flesh of animals, it is "all plants that bear seed everywhere on the earth, and every tree bearing fruit which yields seed: they shall be yours for food". (Genesis 1:29, NEB).

'Now I do not believe the message regarding what was to serve as food for humans in the most perfect state of creation could be any clearer. Genesis clearly presents a picture of veganism; that is, not only is the flesh of animals excluded from the menu God provides for us, even animal products – milk and cheese, for example – are excluded.'[32]

This is similar to C.S. Lewis's belief that it was not only humans who fell from paradise—that we took animals with us and they were reduced to preying on one another. This was his explanation for the cruelty of nature.

The concerns of both historical and present-day Christian scholars go beyond animal welfare and deciding whether animals are conscious, feel pain, or are rational. For many it is a matter of our moral obligation to other creatures.

For centuries moral philosophers have been divided on the subject. Are animals the subjects of a life or are they a bunch of cells that exist, are fed, die and decompose? To Thomas Aquinas animals were incapable of directing their actions; they were mere instruments and therefore needed to be directed by humans. Similarly, Immanuel Kant wrote that they lacked autonomy and will, and were therefore not moral beings; that rationality and autonomy were required to give a creature moral value. It's unclear what he thought about young children, who also lack autonomy and rationality.

As Bil Gilbert wrote, 'So much depends upon the assumption of man's being the only rational animal, capable of intelligent behaviour, that if the definition were proved false the consequences would radically affect our entire view of the world.'[33]

*

Tom Regan says that the further removed an animal is from a caring human, the less it seems to matter what becomes of them. There are examples of this all around us: the way some animals become sentimental favourites—whales, for example—and there is much chest-beating about their fate, while other animals—like intensively farmed pigs—rarely make it to the front page. Some animals are protected by our sentimentality, while others are sacrificed because of our blindness.

People who believe that humans have no direct duty to animals do not necessarily mean that it is okay to hurt them. For some, an animal's right to protection is an indirect right, due to their relationship to some human. Hurting the animal would offend the human who owns or cares about them and that is wrong.

The key to this value of rights is that morality is essentially a set of values that humans sign up to. Those who can sign the contract abide by its rules and are protected by them. Animals, of course, can't sign contracts so they don't count. Regan argues that using this argument as a basis for ethics leaves the way wide open for abuse to occur and, taken to its logical conclusion, not just to animals. It doesn't work as a theory of justice with humans. For example, if one harmed a child or intellectually disabled person this would clearly be wrong, whether or not such an act upset some other person who might be covered by the 'contract'. As in such cases, so too with animals. Harming the animal is *wrong in itself*. According to Regan: 'The fundamental wrong is the system that allows us to view animals as our resources, here for us—to be eaten, or surgically manipulated, or exploited for sport or money. Once we accept this view of animals—as our resources—the rest is as predictable as it is regrettable.'[34]

*

The influential American philosopher John Rawls, in his seminal work *A Theory of Justice*, believed that the best rules for creating and governing a just society were those that would be chosen from behind a veil of ignorance. Those that people would choose without self-interest because they don't know what their 'self' is. In this way, it would be possible to guarantee that any social contract entered into would be 'fair'. Rawls believed animals were not a party to this, that they did not have rights because they were incapable of entering into such a social contract, but others have argued that his theory lends itself to an extension to animals: that if the 'veil of ignorance' included ignorance of species membership, then the architecture of the society that was agreed upon would include equal rights for animals.

Although Rawls excluded animals from his theory of justice, he did believe humans had a moral duty towards them, one that required us to be compassionate and which recognised that animals were sentient creatures with various interests, such as freedom from suffering. What distinguishes Rawls from other philosophers, such as Tom Regan and Peter Singer, who have taken the cause of animals further, is his denial of animal *rights*.

A common argument against animal rights has been that only rational, autonomous and self-conscious beings deserve full, equal moral status. And since only human beings are rational, autonomous and self-conscious, it follows that only human beings deserve full and equal moral status.

Singer has attacked this attitude from several angles. One is that if only humans deserve full and equal moral status, there must be some quality that all humans have that all animals lack. Such things as rationality, autonomy and self-consciousness may be held by most people but they are often absent in children and the intellectually impaired. So if we deny rights to animals on the basis that they lack these qualities, then we should deny rights to such humans as well. This is known as the 'argument from marginal cases'; one wishes the philosophers had come up with a less objectionable name. The argument is that if it is not considered reasonable to deny rights to children or intellectually impaired people, nor should rights be denied to animals.

Singer builds his theory around 'interests'. It is commonly held that the interests of animals are of less significance than those of humans. But on what basis? If it is because they lack those qualities outlined above, then the 'argument from marginal cases' comes into play. For Singer, if we give unequal consideration of interests to animals, then we will be forced to concede unequal consideration of interests to some human beings as well.

Singer's position is considered to be utilitarian, in that he is interested in equality but also utility—the greatest good for the greatest number. Singer's 'equal consideration of interests' leads him to consider situations where it might be acceptable for an animal, which has lived a good life, to die so that many people can eat the meat. It is a balance of interests. For this he has been criticised by other animal rights campaigners, including Tom Regan.

According to Regan, the utilitarian does not value the individual, only the individual's interests. He says, 'The utilitarian's position leads to results that impartial people find morally callous.' Singer has been repeatedly attacked by disability advocates, who believe that his version of the 'argument from marginal cases' would see severely disabled babies left to die, presumably because they have no more right to life than an animal. Singer is just being intellectually consistent, but one can see Regan's point.

To Singer, the capacity for suffering and the capacity for happiness and the enjoyment of life is the fundamental interest that entitles a being to equal consideration. He sees a life—animal or human—as a journey; and the taking of life as wrong if it frustrates the goal of that journey. Some frustrations can be tolerated (and expected) but because it is a journey, the individual who has embarked upon it is not replaceable. They have a personal interest in remaining alive.

Although the arguments of philosophers can seem dense and removed from reality, they do require us to think hard about the hard-to-think-about. Animal behaviourists have revealed to us levels of rationality, autonomy and self-consciousness far beyond our expectations; they and the philosophers force us to think about the animals around us and our responsibility towards them.

Chapter 13
The Implications of Consciousness

For centuries animals were viewed as dumb brutes, not able to speak, not able to think. Language was seen as the magic attribute that separated us from them. While for most of the twentieth century, scientists derided the notion of animal consciousness, in the latter part of the century scientists gradually uncovered the special talents of all sorts of animals. But recognising that animals have consciousness is a huge step for humans, and dangerous, too, as it might well undermine not only traditional thinking but much of our traditional eating.

While the position of animals, their place in the universe and our responsibility towards them has been a perpetual question for philosophers, mostly their conclusions have not been to animals' advantage. The idea of the food chain, a hierarchy of value, originated with St Thomas Aquinas and his belief in animals as mere instruments of humans. Then there was Immanuel Kant who said that because animals lacked autonomy and rationality, they had no moral value. And Rene Descartes, who denied animal consciousness on the basis that it was not necessary to believe in animals' awareness to explain their behaviour. Human belief that animals don't suffer—or at least not as *we* suffer—has justified much.

Peter Singer's work draws heavily on that of the eighteenth-century philosopher Jeremy Bentham, considered the founder of utilitarianism, whose most influential line on animals was: 'The question is not, Can they reason? Nor, Can they talk? But, Can they suffer?'

So what is 'suffering'? The American Veterinary Medical Association lists it as:

Pain—an unpleasant sensory and emotional experience associated with damage to tissues

Distress—a state in which an animal is unable to adapt to an altered environment (e.g. abnormal food) or altered internal states

Discomfort—a state in which the animal seems unadapted to a new environment. These might be physical or social changes and are indicated by changes in physiology and behaviour

Anxiety—a state of increased arousal and alertness prompted by an unknown danger, such as a cat might experience on a visit to a vet

Fear—a response to a known danger present in the immediate environment.

But is killing the same as suffering? This is the belief of American law professor and animal rights theorist Gary Francione. Francione, author of *Eat Like You Care* and *Introduction to Animal Rights*, believes, like Tom Regan, that animals have the right not to be treated as a human resource—the right not to be treated as the property of humans.

Francione says animal sentience and the things animals will do to avoid danger or pain or death prove that they value life; therefore killing them is a violation of their rights. This is in contrast to Peter Singer, who believes that humanely killing an animal that has been well cared for and well treated can be justified. For him, persuading people to eat less meat, rather than no meat, is more achievable and therefore more effective in reducing animal exploitation.

*

Some who write about these things have had very little exposure to real, living animals. In a way I envy them. I imagine how one's ideas and passions could take flight, propelled by the avalanche of material available when one starts to lift the lid on the way animals are treated. It would be like being part of the civil rights movement all over again, with right all on one side. And yet...

Regan says that the first wrong we do is to consider that these living creatures are resources that we have the right to use. That is the first sin. After that, it's a slippery slide of factory farms, conveyor belts, overcrowding, deformities, antibiotic-laced feed and, finally, a messy and often botched death. For him, the way to avoid the slippery slide is not to commit the first sin.

We now consider humans to be resources, enshrined in the departmental nomenclature of every corporation. The human resources hired to do a job can work or resign, or maybe go on strike. If the sow in the sow crate goes on strike, she will be killed. Like a slave, she cannot resign.

On family farms they might be treated well, but they can't just leave. On the other hand, if the gate were left open they probably wouldn't leave anyway. It could be because the paddock provides familiarity and security and feed. But it could also be that generations of enforced helplessness have removed their capacity to enjoy liberty. Given that, it could be argued that it is better to take care of them; that a farmer is a caretaker.

Unlike in the United States and much of Europe, where the vast majority of cattle live on factory farms known as feedlots, in Australia 64 per cent of cattle are still paddock raised and fattened. But that percentage is dropping.

In *Eating Animals*, Jonathan Safran Foer writes of the time well before factory farms when farmers living not much above subsistence level raised and killed animals with care, deliberation and frugality. The farmer was the giver of life and the taker, and both were done in moderation. Now billions of pigs and chickens are raised and eaten annually. It is not only that populations have grown—a lot more of us simply eat a lot more meat. Even in my lifetime I remember when a roast chicken dinner was an occasion. Not any more. Now, farming animals is an industry and chickens roll off the factory floor in vast numbers, treated as insentient, edible things.

The philosophical position of Descartes, who thought animals should be viewed as machines, has in Safran Foer's opinion become a reality, as factory farms raise billions of animals for slaughter. But actually it is not the animals that have become the machines, it is the humans who farm them. Humans have suppressed any empathy they may feel towards other living creatures so as to treat them as a commodity. The vast numbers that abattoirs process and the repetitive nature of the work means that abattoir workers become as desensitised as machines.

One former abattoir worker described this process, telling the BBC: 'One skill that you master while working at an abattoir is disassociation. You learn to become numb to death and to suffering. Instead of thinking about cows as entire beings, you separate them into their saleable, edible body parts. It doesn't just make the job easier—it's necessary for survival.' Nonetheless, what the worker witnessed during the day would return to haunt her. 'At night, my mind would taunt me with nightmares, replaying some of the horrors I'd witnessed throughout the day.'[35]

Such work may take a toll on the mental health of abattoir employees. Depression, anxiety, aggression and higher levels of crime, antisocial behaviour and sexual offending have been reported in recent studies.[36] Some researchers have hypothesised that constantly witnessing and participating in the slaughter of animals may produce a form of trauma referred to perpetration-induced traumatic stress disorder. It is a form of post-traumatic stress disorder whereby the person is involved, or believes they are involved, in creating the traumatic situation.[37]

An abattoir is an environment that breeds brutality, so that even when 'humane' practices are meant to be followed, there is institutionalised carelessness that leads to appalling suffering. Australians witnessed the cruelty inflicted on cattle exported to Indonesian abattoirs a few years ago. Documented in an ABC TV program, it showed Australian cattle being whipped, beaten, slashed and in immense pain before slaughter. The sight of one steer trembling as he watched others being slaughtered ahead of him is not easily forgotten.[38]

Closer to home, the treatment of retired racehorses has raised concerns. Anyone who assumed that these thoroughbreds were all being rehomed and spending their sunset years in grassy paddocks would have been shocked to discover some were being sent to abattoirs. In one infamous Queensland case, the horses were being beaten, kicked and shocked with electric prods when they got there.[39]

One can't leave the blame at the abattoir door: all of us who eat meat are complicit. We are all, as Safran Foer says, 'farming by proxy'.

The practices of factory farming are in a different league altogether from traditional farming, where the health and wellbeing of the animals were a farmer's principal concern. Regan is critical of the idea that one can eat animals ethically. For him, treating animals as a resource that we can use and eat is wrong, no matter how well they are cared for. But given that humans have always eaten meat when they can get it (with a few exceptions), I'm not prepared to be too hardline. The it's-okay-to-eat-happy-animals position is highly contested. For starters, how does one know for sure that the chicken one is eating really did have a good life? The terms 'free range' and even 'organic' are not much of a guarantee. And Safran Foer makes a good point when he says that the effort of deciding, at every meal, what you should or shouldn't eat becomes so wearying that it becomes in the end easier to make the simple decision not to eat animal products and stick to it.

But I am nowhere near ready for that position, so I struggle on with being a selective omnivore. At the moment I have pretty much ruled out chicken and pork. That was easy. But I am still eating beef and sometimes lamb, although I struggle with that. Why isn't mutton more readily available? Our settler ancestors lived on the stuff. And I still eat eggs (our own) and milk and fish—even though I know what goes on in the fishing industry, the enormous wastefulness of modern fishing methods. I have, however, been forced to give up salmon because they, too, are factory farmed and at enormous cost to the Tasmanian environment.

Safran Foer writes of two rare farmers he has come to know who farm traditionally—Frank farms turkeys, Paul farms pigs. He admires them both, not least for holding out against the huge corporate enterprises that so dominate US agriculture. He believes they look after their animals well and are passionate about doing so. Indeed, they have dedicated their lives to that end. But still, he says he can't eat the pork or turkey they produce. Other factors come into the process of getting a happy pig from the farm where it has lived its life to your dinner plate. Pigs are castrated, not a happy experience. They are transported long distances (much further than used to be the case, because of the disappearance of local abattoirs) and that is frightening and stressful for them. And eating meat of any kind increases the demand for meat and thereby indirectly supports factory farming.

He writes: 'Different people will draw the line in different places with regard to farms like Paul's and Frank's. People I respect draw it differently. But for me, for now—for my family now—my concerns about the reality of what meat is and has become are enough to make me give it up altogether.'[40]

Eating is such an automatic thing. But when you come to care about these things, it becomes a constant exercise in remembering and forgetting. We all 'remember' our favourite flavours; go to them automatically on a menu. But now, when I go to a menu, it is a different kind of remembering that I do. And when, as sometimes happens, I find that I have eaten some animal product that I now would normally not do, I am reminded of what it was that I temporarily forgot. To enjoy the kind of meal I used to relish is now an exercise in forgetting.

If one concedes that animals have souls, is eating one akin to cannibalism? We've had to convince ourselves of animals' limitations so as to give ourselves permission to use them as we do. If we actually concede that they are soulful, self-aware 'subjects of a life', it puts us in a very awkward position.

PART TWO

PART TWO

Chapter 14
Bird Brains

'Alex taught me to believe that his little bird brain was conscious in some manner; that is, capable of intention. By extrapolation, Alex taught me that we live in a world populated by thinking, conscious creatures. Not human thinking. Not human consciousness. But not mindless automatons sleepwalking through their lives, either.'[41]

This is how scientist Dr Irene Pepperberg wrote about her African grey parrot Alex, the most famous parrot in history. Alex died in 2007 after working with Pepperberg in her laboratory for thirty years. 'Brainy parrot dies, emotive to the end' was the way *The New York Times* announced Alex's demise. It noted how Alex had learned more than 100 words, knew his colours and shapes, and how his last words to Pepperberg as she put him in the cage the night before he died were: 'You be good, see you tomorrow. I love you.'

Alex's abilities during his life had made him an international avian celebrity. His demise was covered by *Time* magazine, *The Guardian*, CNN, PBS and even *The Economist*.

When Pepperberg began working with Alex she had no idea that the bird she bought from a pet store as a one year old was going to help overturn human understanding of the capabilities of non-human animals.

Alex not only learned words; he appeared to understand what they meant. He could name objects, such as a key, no matter its size or colour. He challenged the notion that parrots are capable only of mimicking words. Pepperberg was convinced that Alex knew exactly what he was saying. If he asked for a grape and was given a banana, he would spit it back and repeat his demand for a grape.[42] At times he coined new words to describe unfamiliar objects. He called an apple a 'banerry' the first time he was shown one—possibly because its creamy inside resembled a banana and its outside a cherry—fruits he was already familiar with and could name.

He could express frustration. Tired after repeating some trials dozens of times, he would throw objects off the trays with his beak.

Until Alex, birds were not believed to possess the potential for language or consciousness. Alex challenged that notion and showed how ill-informed and dismissive is the term 'bird brain'. Alex showed what fond pet owners have long suspected: that a lot is going on inside an animal, and we can only guess the half of it.

*

A few years ago, several hundred delegates from more than twenty countries descended on Newcastle, New South Wales, to take part in the largest animal studies conference ever held. It comprised a diverse range of people and subjects: philosophers, scientists, animal rights activists and historians. A dizzying array of papers were delivered in five, and sometimes six, simultaneous sessions every hour for six days. The import was that this will be the century when humankind strikes a new deal with the animal kingdom.

The conference, entitled Minding Animals, was held at the City Hall, a wonderful 1930s edifice that seems to exude confidence about human achievements and satisfaction with our place in the world as the pre-eminent species. The academics and activists who took over its concert hall, meeting rooms, banquet rooms and supper rooms were—for all the differences in opinion—highly tolerant of each other. So broad was the range of interests on show that delegates were more inclined to show curiosity towards one another than the kind of savagery common in more tightly bound disciplines.

There is no one academic area that covers 'animal studies'. It is a sprawling subject that spills over from ethology (animal behaviour) into biology, psychology, geography, neuro and cognitive science, veterinary science and more. And then there are the humanities subjects—history, literature, religion, philosophy—where animals crop up constantly as soon as you start to look. There is so much going on in animal studies that it seems inevitable that it will change the way that humans view non-human animals. Already it is beginning to affect what we eat and how we farm animals.

Philosophers are at the forefront of much of the work being done. Peter Singer, whose 1976 book *Animal Liberation* became a founding text of the animal rights movement, told the conference that over the past thirty years philosophers had challenged people to re-examine their beliefs about animals; in particular to recognise the 'cognitive overlap' between humans and animals. On the matter of eating them, he said it was unrealistic...would reduce animal suffering.

The food at the conference was vegan, and this was popular even among the meat eaters. It is not possible to sit for hours hearing about the lives of animals then turn around and eat one. I took my first steps towards vegetarianism at that conference. I don't think I will ever become a strict vegetarian but it made me start to think about what I eat, and once you start to do that you find there are a lot of dishes that you simply have no appetite for: chickens, for example, the ones that have been grown fat and fast, six weeks from birth to death, in vast broiler sheds, their little skeletons unable to support the artificial growth that is forced upon them. Or pork, from an industry where sows are piglet machines and spend their lives in cages so small they cannot turn around in them.

It is now widely accepted that animals do feel pain but the degree of that ability to feel/know/perceive—their sentience and cognisance—is still contested territory. Apes and dolphins, maybe, but lizards? The work that has been done over recent decades has exploded many myths. We now know that the individuals of many species recognise one another, communicate with one another, feel distress and sorrow. Maybe even lizards, although the jury is still out on that one.

At a session entitled 'Attending to animals', on feminism and animal studies, the point was made that feminism has had little to say about animals. Perhaps this is because, as soon as you start 'attending to animals', concepts like care, nurturing, attentiveness and consideration arise. In the early years of feminism, these were concepts that women were keen to untether from preconceptions of what it is to be a woman.

But times have moved on. Instead of worrying about our relationships with men, some of us are beginning to worry about our relationships with animals. Being attentive to animals, and recognising the relationships we have with them, unveils a new world view – the start, perhaps, of another revolution. The first step is recognising that each animal is the subject of its own life.

Humans sleep to restore our brains after the demands of a day of conscious life. Frogs and other animals that probably aren't conscious don't seem to sleep. But mammals and birds do sleep and maybe that is because they, too, need a break from their conscious lives. And maybe they also wake, as we do, and, as American anthropologist Matt Cartmill writes, 'experience their presence in the world'.

Cartmill says, 'Sleep seems to restore something that is damaged or depleted by things that go on in our brains when we are conscious.' And it may well be the same for other animals.[43] He writes: 'The British psychologist C. Lloyd Morgan laid down the following law in 1894: "In no case may one interpret an action as the outcome of the exercise of a higher psychical faculty, if it can be interpreted as the outcome of the exercise of one which stands lower in the psychological scale."

'For Morgan, "higher" implicitly meant "human". Psychologists today revere his dictum under the name of Morgan's Canon. Why do they so readily accept it? Why is it safer to assume that human brain functions are unique? People who study kidney evolution don't think it's anthropomorphic to interpret an animal's urine as the outcome of the exercise of higher (humanlike) kidney faculties.'

According to Cartmill: 'Just as we anthropomorphize dogs, horses, and other domestic animals, they return the favour by using their own social signals to greet, entreat, and threaten us and each other—much as they would fellow members of their species. Scientists often regard this "assimilation tendency" in animals as some sort of mistake, as if the poor stupid beasts were confusing dogs, horses, and people. But if all these similar species have similar mental lives, the assimilation tendency is perfectly realistic.'

Perhaps, 'Our ancestors evolved consciousness because it enabled them "to read the minds of others by reading their own".' If so, why deny the possibility that other animals might have done the same? Cartmill says such skills would be very useful to all sorts of animals: 'A zebra that can tell when a lion is feeling hungry is less likely to get eaten. A dog or a man who can tell when a horse is furiously angry is less likely to get kicked in the head. Insofar as anthropomorphism alerts us to the mental states of other species, it's not a mistake; it's a survival skill.'

Alex the parrot was able to prove that he could think and feel. On one occasion, Pepperberg was demonstrating to a visiting colleague some of the things of which Alex was capable: distinguishing between objects and counting. It had become clear to Pepperberg that Alex sometimes got bored (as well he might given that he sometimes had to repeat an experiment hundreds of times for it to be scientific). On this particular day, Alex was not being cooperative. He was shown a range of objects in groups: three of this, four of that etc. and was asked a question, the answer to which was 'two'. But he repeatedly gave every answer except 'two'. So Pepperberg told him, 'Okay, you're going back in your room.' She put him away in his room and closed the door. As she walked away, Alex immediately began calling out, 'Two... two...I'm sorry. Come back!'

*

Over the past couple of decades a gradual change has come over researchers working in the area of animal cognition, a growing realisation that in refusing to acknowledge that animals might have the ability to make choices, to remember, to think through their actions—in other words to refuse to recognise that animals might have *minds*—they were throwing the baby out with the bath water. Where could all their research take them if they refused to consider the possibility that animals think?

The American Donald Griffin was one of the first and most influential to break ranks. The prominent zoologist believed that while intelligent and complex behaviour is not necessarily conscious, there is no need for us to rule out the possibility of consciousness in animals. He believed that many animals could think, remember, anticipate and intend. And for many years he was derided for it. But he persevered, publishing several books, including *Animal Minds* and *Animal Thinking*. By the time he died in 2003 the tide had well and truly begun to turn in his direction.

Now there is a growing plethora of books that take up the battle for fuller recognition to be given to animals for their consciousness, their cultures and their moralities; books like Steven Wise's *Rattling the Cage: Towards Legal Rights for Animals* and Marc Bekoff and Jessica Pierce's *Wild Justice: The Moral Lives of Animals*, to name just two.

This next generation of books, following on from earlier seminal works of the animal rights movement, like Peter Singer's *Animal Liberation*, not only tell us empirically about developments in research into animal behaviour; they offer a philosophical challenge to alter our thinking about what animals are.

Steven Wise believes that apes should be given rights analogous to those of humans because they are conscious, intelligent beings, not all that dissimilar from us. He has fought for many years for apes to be granted 'personhood'. Some countries have done so, New Zealand and Spain for example. Indeed, New Zealand was the first country to do so back in 1999, prompted by a group of scientists and conservationists who argued that great apes shared many emotional and psychological characteristics with humans, including self-awareness and the ability to reason.

Wise runs an organisation called the Nonhuman Rights Project and they have been campaigning in the US for apes and elephants kept in captivity. His work was the subject of a 2016 documentary *Unlocking the Cave*, by high-profile directors Chris Hegedus and D.A. Pennebaker (*The War Room, Don't Look Back*).

Wise's argument is a legal one, that in withholding such rights, human-made law is violating natural law. One English reviewer, the prolific English writer and commentator Kenan Malik, dismissed this, saying that 'no animal possesses either language or a social network *like ours* [my emphasis]...to have a right means also to be responsible for one's actions, to be recognised as a moral being'. He went on to say, in effect, that because animals' social organisation was unlike ours they were unworthy of legal protection. It sounds an awful lot like the kind of rationalisations that were often used to deny rights to Indigenous people. And it ignores that most species have their own kind of social organisation and that we humans are only at the start of discovering the degree of consciousness involved in animal social organisation.

Chapter 15
What Is 'Natural' to Animals?

There is a lot of common and well-meaning nonsense about what is 'natural' to animals, as if human beings are the only ones that adapt to circumstances, or can make choices, or have individual likes and dislikes.

We may not be able to *know* what an animal is thinking but we can make an effort to find out, using observation, comparison where appropriate, and some initial guesswork backed up by experimentation.

The other day, at my friend Sally's, Vincent was showing a great deal of interest in a small tabby cat that was sitting on a chair in the saddle-up area. Vincent approached the cat and reached his nose down to her. The cat reached her nose up to Vincent. Then she bowed her head and rubbed her forehead against his muzzle. I could see her pleasurably leaning her weight into it. Then Vincent began nuzzling her fur with his lip. The cat sat still and allowed him to run his muzzle all over her head, neck and shoulders. He kept this up for some minutes, using his lip to explore her. He seemed to particularly enjoy the sensation of her fur on the skin between his nostrils.

She has grown up with horses, so had no fear. But what did Vincent think he was up to? He does like having his muzzle rubbed, so perhaps it was simply that. But I think it had to do, too, with the texture of the cat's fur. It may even have been a display of affection or curiosity or an exchange of scents as a precursor to friendship. I've noticed in the past that he seems to quite like cats.

The motion he was making with his lips was very like that which horses use when they are scratching each other's necks and backs: I wonder if he was actually asking for a scratch? If I had thought of that at the time I could have given him one, as the cat could not—or at least, not the sort he was asking for!

A lot of research is being done in social neuroscience about animal play: what prompts them to play and what feelings it creates in them. Researchers have found that when rat pups play, there is a release of hormones into the brain that create feelings of happiness, comfort and pleasure. In other words, the play produced the pleasure.

The internet is full of clips of animals at play for what appears to be the sheer fun of it. There's the baby goat sliding repeatedly down a stone ramp in India, an Australian Shepherd in the snow dragging a plastic sledge up a hill, climbing aboard and tobogganing down, over and over again.

What do creatures get out of playing? Is there purpose to their activity or is it simply a joyful diversion? Some have speculated that play helps animals learn survival skills. Yet the jury is out on this. Cats raised without toys, for example, were no less able to catch mice than cats raised with toy mice and balls of yarn, one study found.[44]

*

For years I noticed that when our dogs came inside of an evening they almost always started playing together. It was the time of the day when we all sat down together in the living room. The humans relaxed and watched a bit of television and the dogs enjoyed their special 'indoor time'. They had their own mat behind the sofa and would roll around on it together, mock fighting, growling and chewing at each other. Sometimes their playful growls and yelps were so loud we couldn't hear the TV and would have to hush them. To me this playfulness was a sign of comfort and joy at being all together in a safe, warm place. The comfort and joy *produced* the play, or so I always felt.

To come to their conclusion about play producing pleasure, neuroscientists had to slice an awful lot of rat brains. And, unfortunately, they couldn't slice the rats' brains open and then let them play. So they concluded that the play produced the happy hormones they found in the brains. But I am still convinced our dogs were happy—and that is what made them play.

But then nature is full of such chicken and egg conundrums.

*

When it comes to horses, not a great deal is really known—as in scientifically proven. The experiments that have been undertaken have mostly been fairly basic. Some misconceptions have been disproved, such as that horses are colourblind. They are not but they do see a smaller range of colours than we do. They are believed to have red/green blindness, as do many people.

Common wisdom among equine behaviourists has held that they are not very intelligent, that they are driven by 'instinct', whatever that means—more on that later. At the other end of the spectrum, horse enthusiasts influenced by New Age ideas attribute great intelligence to their horses. Some researchers have devised various experiments to show the extent, or limitation, of horse intelligence. Here in Australia, Andrew McLean has used his bucket experiment to show that horses cannot hold information in their brains. The experiment consists of placing a horse and handler at one point on an imaginary triangle, and two assistants with buckets at the other two points of the triangle. One of the assistants pours feed into their bucket. If the horse is released immediately it will go straight to the bucket with the feed in it. If there is a delay between the pouring of the feed and the release of the horse of ten seconds or more, the horse as often as not goes to the wrong bucket. It is a simple experiment, perhaps too simple.

One problem I have with it is the conclusion drawn by McLean: that horses are not very intelligent. Yet at the same time, he says, and we all know, that horses have very good memories. If he is correct, and horses cannot 'remember' which bucket is holding the feed, how is it that they can remember frightening experiences they have had or, more pertinently, lessons they have been taught, months, even years later? McLean says it is because 'recall' of a particular just-passed moment is not the same as remembering cues that have been repeated many times. His experiment proves, he says, that horses don't have 'object permanence'.

Although the bucket experiment is simple, there is a complicating factor: the three humans who are in the experiment with the horse. How might that affect the horse's response? In Germany there was a famous horse called Clever Hans whose trainer, Wilhelm von Osten, swore could count. Time after time horse and handler would demonstrate this amazing ability, with Hans tapping out the correct number with his hoof. Even sceptics began to believe that the horse could indeed count. Then it was discovered that Hans only got the number right if von Osten knew the answer. If von Osten didn't know, then suddenly Hans couldn't count. He had been picking up on minute cues from his (no doubt beloved) handler—his eyes, the muscles of his face. Some clue, given unconsciously by the handler, was enough to let Hans know that it was time to stop tapping with his hoof. When this was deduced, it was said that Clever Hans wasn't clever at all. But how dumb is that! He was able to pick up on signs invisible to the human eye. Body language, or maybe even telepathic signals.

I believe it is in comparing 'intelligence' between horses and humans that McLean's hypothesis breaks down; there, and in his insistence on being 'objective', which denies the animal's right to subjectivity. McLean's intention is to remove sentiment and woolly thinking from people's dealings with horses, 'for the sake of the horse'. He is tired of people blaming the horse for bad behaviour, believing there is no such thing as a 'bad horse', only a horse that has not been given clear and consistent signals and so has become confused. (Can an unintelligent animal be confused?) Yet in being intent on 'scientific objectivity', it seems to me he has tied his own hands, much in the way of the old school of animal behaviourists.

American equine researcher Evelyn Hanggi approaches similar questions from the opposite perspective. She wants to show that horses are more cognisant and perceptive than has generally been credited. In her experiments, she removes humans from the equation so that they cannot influence her subjects. The horse learns to cooperate with the experiment, where he is in a specially built room by himself, through positive reinforcement, that is, he receives a reward of food when he gets the answer correct. Her experiments have shown that horses can distinguish between various objects and shapes, and that they can communicate information perceived by one eye to the other eye, something that for a long time was thought not to occur. This is interesting but I'm not sure how much further it takes us. It doesn't get us any closer to understanding what it is to be a horse, or what other abilities they may have.

I found the most interesting part of her experiments to be not the actual experiment but how the horse cooperated. He would wait behind a barrier until the barrier was withdrawn and he could walk forward to the wall where the objects were displayed. After making his choice, and receiving a reward down a chute if it was correct, he would turn, walk down the side of the room, turn again and position himself behind the barrier, ready for the next experiment. All this on his own with no person present. According to Hanggi, the horses learnt this routine in no time.

It brings to mind a question that has always fascinated me: why do they cooperate with us? Why, for example, do most of them readily walk into a horse trailer? Anyone who has ever ridden in a trailer will know that it is a noisy, jolting experience, unnerving for a human, let alone a horse. Why do they do it? McLean would no doubt quote 'learning theory' and the nine steps in his training method. But in the end it comes down to this large animal doing what we want. Perhaps McLean is right, and a cooperative horse is all about the consistency and talent of the trainer. And yet...and yet...

Hanggi's experiments show that horses can distinguish between different shapes and sizes. But gets me no closer to understanding just what it is that Vincent can see from his stable door which so fascinates him.

Paul McGreevy from the Sydney University Veterinary School believes that 'misunderstanding a horse's cognitive abilities has important implications not only for its training program, but also for its welfare. There are negative welfare implications both in overestimating and underestimating mental abilities in animals.'[45] Like most equine behaviourists, McGreevy relies heavily on the small size of the prefrontal cortex of a horse's brain, compared with humans, to support the argument regarding their lack of intelligence. But the African grey parrot Alex seems to have disproved the idea that a 'bird brain', a small brain, is a determinant of intelligence.

*

Charlie is becoming more and more delightful and seems to win everyone's hearts. He is such a sociable cat. Strangers do not faze him at all. The other day, Paul the builder was here to fix the back door, which meant kneeling on the ground beside it. Charlie came up and lay right beside his knees while he worked. And yesterday I was sitting on the ground in the orchard, keeping an eye on Vincent and Jim who were grazing on the tasty green grass, and Charlie came and stretched himself out beside me. He has no fear of the horses.

I'd let the two geldings into the orchard because the grass in the paddocks is burning away to nothing, so hot has it been every day. They say it is the hottest, driest summer in the highlands for twenty-eight years. Certainly I've never seen our place looking so brown. Hard to believe that only a couple of months ago we were saying what a great season we were having, and everywhere was lush and green. I'm going to have to order in hay for the cattle, and I'm very glad we sold the older steers when we did. They fetched a good price, too—over a thousand dollars for Plucky!

Bill has taken to his new role as a stud and is now looking quite the imposing bull—amazing what getting the testosterone moving can do to a bloke's physique! He and the cows and the young steers have settled together nicely but they, too, are starting to notice the reduced fodder. Whenever they see me coming in the ATV all the cows start running towards me, hoping for hay.

Bill's mother, Freckle, has her own little herd now, the idea being to keep Bill from mating with his mother or the young heifers. So as well as her new little son there is one of the other cows who has a heifer calf still at foot, plus the yearling, Peggy Sue. Yesterday when I went for a ride on Vincent I had to leave the gate to the driveway open. The cows were a long way off—two paddocks away. But, sure enough, when I went back half an hour later to shut the gate I was too late. They had discovered it and were already halfway down the next paddock.

It was slightly cooler this morning with some cloud cover so I took the chance to give Vincent a workout in the arena. He and Jim had already been put out in their paddock but Vinnie came back in happily enough. He does seem to enjoy being worked. This morning he was quite hot and sweaty by the end—it was humid and warmed up rapidly—but he stayed cheerful. His ears pricked and his expression was alert at the end of the session.

I hosed him down and rubbed his face, which he does like, and started to think about horse happiness and our responsibility to make sure they are happy. When I was young and had horses, even though I doted on them, I never really considered whether they were happy or not. Now it is something I wonder often. Perhaps I used to assume, as was the fashion, that horses didn't really feel, or at least not as we do. I know their mental and social life is very different to ours, but it seems to me that certain emotions are very recognisable. Crankiness, fear, boredom. A while back I tried out a horse that I was thinking of buying, but in the end there was something about his personality that I didn't take to. He had spent a very large part of his life living in an enormous barn with a lot of other horses, hardly ever getting time outside. It had soured him.

There is a lot of debate now about whether we confine our horses too much; how they are better off living as naturally as possible. I am sure there is a lot in that but I think, too, that what is 'natural' for a horse is not an absolute. They, like us, are a product of their environment. We need to take into account their physiological needs—to move around a lot and kick up their heels occasionally, to stretch their neck to the ground to graze on green shoots, to roll in the dirt, and run with the wind in their mane. But they grow accustomed to the lives they lead with us; we are not insignificant in their universe. Having taken them from the wild, we have a responsibility to befriend them.

Our horses are accustomed to coming in at night—being put in a yard or a stable, getting a nice feed and spending the night enclosed. There are several reasons we do this, not all of them obvious. Most people in Australia leave their horses in paddocks and would say the horses are happier for it. Certainly if you start locking up a horse that has always been in a large paddock, it will make its displeasure clear, circling the stable endlessly, pawing the ground, gnawing on anything it can get a grip on. Such horses are not used to being stabled and are objecting to what seems unnatural. But our animals never behave like this. They are used to the stable, it is part of their routine, they are—dare I say it—happy about it.

I had a friend here recently who doesn't stable or confine her horses and I don't think she approves that I do. So I watched our horses for a few weeks to see if their routine made them unhappy. The other evening, Susan opened the gate of the bottom paddock to let Chelsea and the donkey through so they could come up to the barn—they were prancing around the gate, anxious for her to open it. As soon as she did, Chelsea galloped up towards the barn full tilt, slowed marginally as she approached, and ran straight into the stable, which I had opened for her. Because she is so fat, Chelsea gets only a couple of small dippers of chaff for her dinner and she would be in the stable for twelve hours—and she couldn't wait to get in there!

A few times when Vincent has been away from home and forced to live in a paddock twenty-four hours a day, he hasn't thrived. It seems to make him anxious. Whereas when he lives in a more confined, more social environment, he is secure and therefore happier. During the equine flu epidemic, he was stranded away from home. He was living at a farm where he was very well looked after, yet where he never completely settled. When he was not able to come home because of the flu epidemic we arranged for him to go instead to my friend Sally's. He had lived at Sally's several times before. She keeps her horses in small paddocks during the day and they are stabled at night. It is a routine that Vincent seems happy with. The first afternoon when he arrived at Sally's she put him into one of the day paddocks. Vincent immediately lay down and stretched out full length in the sun. This is a very vulnerable situation for a horse and not one they will get into unless they are feeling very secure.

When our horses come in at night they are all together (whereas they are in pairs in the paddocks during the day), and they get handled as well as fed. It is a relaxed, convivial time of day. A time everyone enjoys, humans and equines. Susan, Jan and I chat and the horses eat. Susan brushes Lina and Lina enjoys it so much that she leans into the brush and stops eating until the grooming is finished. Savouring her pleasures.

If we are running late of an afternoon, they stand at the gates waiting to be brought in. Bringing them in also keeps them off the paddocks for a bit, which, when the season is good, stops them from getting too fat, and when the season is bad, as now, saves the grass from being eaten and trampled twenty-four hours a day.

After I worked him this morning, Vincent stood contentedly while he was hosed, rubbed, had his mane combed and was dressed in paddock boots and rug. His eyes were bright and kindly, his ears pricked. He watched me with an expression that looked to me like happiness as I moved around the barn tidying up. He wasn't restless, he seemed in no hurry to get back out to the paddock. I had the clear impression that he would have stood there while I messed about for hours if that's what I wanted.

Chapter 16
Observing Other Species

Bil Gilbert wrote about his relationship with an aloof and frightened young cheetah called Chief he had been asked to work with at a wildlife park. Their first encounter was not promising. When Gilbert entered Chief's enclosure, the thirty-kilo cat retreated to a corner, ears flattened, formidable fangs exposed, and began hissing. 'Keep away' was the unmistakable message. Gilbert stood motionless before slowly withdrawing, hoping he had at least signalled that he was not hostile.

'Slowly, Chief and I came to trust one another, principally because we were able to establish a rudimentary sort of communication, able to read certain signs and sounds well enough to understand the feelings and wishes of the other. I learned enough cheetah to know how Chief indicated that he was afraid, contented, playful, or bored. He learned enough human to know that I was friendly, that a whistle meant food, "ball" meant a game, and "no" was a command to stop biting. Certainly this was not much of a vocabulary, but it was enough to let us meet in peace, a condition all animals need at times, and a condition which could not be established if animals could not communicate their intentions and desires.'[46]

Much that human beings have learnt about animals has been learnt by observing them – the numbers of researchers who have observed elephants, coyotes, wolves, monkeys, bears, chimpanzees; the trainers of lions and horses and dolphins; the farmers and animal husbanders. Leaving aside for a moment the laboratory experiments—highly artificial situations that often tell more about the experiment and the mind of the experimenter than about the animal—the cumulative experience of millions of people has created our store of knowledge about other species. What we have learnt has often influenced how we behave around them. Not in a bad way: often it has been a productive symbiosis. The hunter with his dog; the horse and rider; the shepherd and flock.

It surprises no one that this is so. So why should it be a radical idea that they also learn about us by observing us? Over thousands of years our behaviour has been modified, and often it has been because of the part some animal has played in our lives that that modification has occurred: the ploughing of fields with bullocks, the drinking of cows' milk, the beginning of long-distance transportation with the horse. Human life is constantly changing, and although we might bemoan the pace of change, as a species we manage it quite well.

So do they. How often we hear people complaining in a disapproving way about animals being handled in a way that is 'not natural'. Animal species that have been in extended contact with humans are altered by that fact, as we have been altered by them. Animals that have been kept in a zoo are not like their wild counterparts, but to say that means that every animal in a zoo is miserable is to misunderstand the individual animal's experience of her own life, and to underestimate her ability to adapt. Does she have company of her own kind? Does she have a friend of her own or another species? Can she move about in a way that her body was designed to do? Does she have food that she likes and which is good for her? These things are crucial and often modern zoos provide them. Does she have an activity that occupies her? This latter is probably the hardest for a zoo to provide.

My point, however, is not about zoos. It is about recognising that an individual animal is not a species and is not entirely limited by the historical living conditions of that species. Like us, they are opportunistic; like us, they learn through experience; like us, they know the difference between pleasure and pain; like us, they can choose.

Yes, through the generations new behaviours learnt under new conditions will evolve to become 'natural' to the species, just as it is now natural for us to walk on two legs. And it may be that this is how at least some of the things we call 'instincts' developed; that they resulted from a learned response repeated over millennia.

There is a difference within species; there are always those individuals who push the boundaries, who are, in Darwin's parlance, 'fittest to survive'. The shifts that occurred within species' behaviour occurred because an individual *changed*. Nowhere is that clearer than with domestication.

Domestication changed animals' behaviour. Whether it changed their nature is another question. And the extent to which it has changed their brain structure we will perhaps never know. They have learnt to live with us: dogs, cats, cows, horses, goats, pigs, chickens. Some species are more human-friendly than others. There are some that, even thousands of years after we began to live together, still have a fear reaction towards humans that has to be ameliorated when they are young—almost as if each new generation has to be domesticated all over again. An individual animal will learn from watching you: the dog who knows what it means when you walk towards a certain cupboard in the kitchen at a certain hour; the cat who knows that when you start picking up and shaking the pillows in the morning, it is time to get off the bed because you are about to make it; the cows who learn when to come to the milking shed.

They also know things we don't know. 'Dogs that know when their owners are coming home', in Rupert Sheldrake's words; the horse who senses trouble around the corner; the elephants who sense an earthquake coming. They learn without being trained, they learn by watching us, they learn because we live together, they learn because they are intelligent, sentient beings. And it seems to me likely that they have learnt more than behaviour. That they have perhaps learnt to understand us, to second-guess us, to know what we are thinking. In my experience of dogs, horses, cats, goats—and, of course, one very special donkey—they have intuitions that far outshine ours. They don't have a sophisticated verbal language like us but how much more sophisticated is their intuition. Instead of blabbering away as we do, they listen, and not only with their ears.

There are so many mysteries in the minds and bodies of non-human animals and we are only beginning to get an inkling of them. The more researchers of many persuasions open up their own, and our, thinking about the nature of animals, the more the mysteries deepen.

One intriguing story among thousands: Petra Stapp, an English researcher looking into the nature of human–animal encounters, was told of an encounter between a woman and a sheep on an English moor. The woman was out walking with her boyfriend. She decided to pause and sit for a while to enjoy the surroundings while her boyfriend walked on. Soon a single sheep appeared over a hill. It walked towards her. Indeed, it walked right up to her, purposefully. She watched. When it reached her, the sheep leant forward and kissed her on the lips. Astonished, the woman sat still. Sheep and woman observed each other, face to face, for a few moments. Then the sheep turned and retraced its steps.

All this was observed by the boyfriend from further along the track. The two finished their walk and returned to the car. The woman switched on her mobile phone and retrieved a message that was left at about the same time as her encounter with the sheep. The message was from a friend, telling her that another close friend had just died.

How do we interpret this encounter?

She was unlikely to be hallucinating because the encounter was observed by a third party. Maybe it was a coincidental meeting with an affectionate sheep. Or perhaps it was, as the woman believed, that the sheep was delivering a final farewell from her dead friend. We have no rational way of accounting for that. It may be that we will never know the truth behind such human–animal interactions. But the abundance of stories like this suggests that our human-centric explanations of animal capability are seriously lacking.

Our lives are so entwined with animals. For thousands of years they have helped us survive in all sorts of ways: dogs who became domesticated and hunted with their humans, a process that benefited both; the cats that enabled people to begin accumulating grain because they controlled rats and mice. Without the ability to store grain, cities may never have developed.

Cats were revered and domesticated in ancient Egypt. An image of a cat staring down a rat was painted on a Middle Kingdom tomb around 2000 years ago. It is believed to be the first image of a domesticated cat in Egyptian art.

The 'beasts of burden' made it possible for human societies to move, trade and conquer. The accidental discovery of a particular type of horse transformed the military might of ancient China. Around 200 BCE, the Han emperor Wudi sent an envoy from China's imperial capital Xian west into uncharted terrain. The envoy eventually reached Ferghana in present-day Uzbekistan. There he encountered creatures he had never seen before: huge, swift, powerful horses. Their astonishing appearance was compounded by the blood that some appeared to sweat (today this is believed to be the result of a parasite). At the time, China possessed only small, hefty horses. When the envoy returned with news of these slender horses, the emperor quickly realised the enormous military advantage they would provide as his dynasty battled nomadic, horse-mounted enemies. He resolved to acquire the Central Asian horses. The Heavenly Horses have long inspired Chinese paintings, poems and statues, including the country's most famous sculpture—the bronze Han dynasty Flying Horse of Gansu, which captures the speed and power of the Heavenly Horse.

Of the beasts of burden, none have been more significant to ancient trade and commerce than the two-humped Bactrian camels. They were essential to the ancient Silk Road, the network of trade routes that connected China with the eastern Mediterranean and the subcontinent. Caravans of Bactrian camels were used for centuries to convey goods, including glass, jade, metals, tea and silk. They were the trucks of the Silk Road. Native to Central Asia, Bactrian camels were suited to extremes of heat and cold encountered en route and capable of traversing not only desert sands but also rocky mountains. Unlike the single-humped Arabian dromedary, the Bactrian camel's thick winter coat protected it in subzero temperatures. Its sealable nostrils kept out the violent spring dust storms to which Central Asia is prone.

Animals have also been used to colonise. There is a little-known example of the latter in our own history, and its ramifications are still being felt by one animal in Australia today. Dromedaries have been romanticised in the Australian story—'ships of the desert'—but alongside them, and outnumbering them, were donkeys. Big teams of fifty or more were used to pull the wagons that took supplies and mail. They moved between towns, stations and settlements. When motorised transport came and they weren't needed any more, the men who used them and cared for them took them out into the bush to some remote well and let them go. The donkeys, being donkeys—smart and adaptable—not only survived but multiplied.

They're what we like to call 'feral', meaning that, having introduced them, we damn them for existing in places adjacent to those we introduced them to. Chased and hunted off the good land, they retreated ever further into the interior. They have the sense to give humans a wide berth.

Aerial culling is widely accepted: the removal of species that are damaging our environment, threatening the livelihood of native animals, and so on. But it becomes more complicated the closer one looks. Once again humans are playing God, deciding which are worthy animals and which are not. It may be that donkeys eat the grass that native animals might eat; but the real problem is that they eat the grass the cattle belonging to pastoralists might otherwise eat.

Since the 1970s donkeys in the Kimberley and the Northern Territory have been culled from the air, hundreds of thousands of them. Since the 1990s the culling has been done in a particularly nasty way. A female, a mature jenny, is captured and fitted with a radio collar, then released. She meets up with a herd and the helicopter shooters track the herd by following her radio signal. All the herd are then shot from the air, bar the jenny with the collar. This collar is known in the trade as a Judas collar, and the donkey who wears it is a Judas donkey, because she then moves on until she finds another group of donkeys to hang out with. The helicopter flies in, all the other donkeys are killed, and the Judas donkey is again alone...until she meets up with the next herd of donkeys. After this happens a few times the Judas jenny ceases looking for friends. She has worked it out: wherever she goes, the others die. From then on she stays alone.

No one who has ever known a donkey could be unaffected by this practice because donkeys are by nature gentle creatures. Researcher Jill Bough found that the shooters were often sad about what they had to do, taking pride only in doing it cleanly. Most of us close our minds to the atrocities that we perpetrate on animals. That is the only way we can carry on as the dominant species and still sleep at night.

Our blindness towards animals reminds me of how colonisers of all races viewed those they colonised. Even the terminology is the same: brutes, dumb animals, uncivilised; meaning they don't live like us, don't have the finer feelings that we have, don't speak our language. As a society we have armed ourselves with prejudices against animals the way we once armed ourselves against Indigenous people (and women). The thousands of academics who have found in 'animal studies' a passionate new home may well be at the forefront of the next revolution.

Chapter 17
Cross-species Empathy and Cooperation

Some time ago, after days of heavy rain which had made riding impossible, I took Vincent in the trailer down to my coach's place to ride him in the indoor arena. There was no one about—everyone was either away or occupied in another part of the property. I rode and then dismounted to lead Vincent back up to the car park. As we walked out of the arena, I stepped in front of him to avoid a puddle, a foolish thing to do. Just at that moment a horse in a nearby paddock startled and broke into a gallop, which frightened Vincent. He leapt forward and knocked me to the ground, then went straight over the top of me. I think he gave himself as big a fright as he gave me. He stopped and looked back at me, lying face down in a large, thankfully soft, muddy puddle. I stood up with difficulty. I was sore and winded. There was mud coating my face, my hair, my clothes. There was so much mud on my glasses that I couldn't see. I caught hold of Vinnie's reins and we made our way slowly up to the car park with me hanging onto his mane for support.

I tied him to the trailer. How the hell was I going to get him unsaddled and load him on the trailer? I could barely stand up! At the stables I called out, trying to find one of the staff. I was moaning and groaning. I cleaned off my glasses as best I could and shook the mud from my hair. Failing to find anyone, I went back to where I'd left Vincent. He turned and eyed me anxiously and did something I've never known him to do before or since: he whinnied a low, *worried* whinny. It was not the sound he occasionally greets me with in the stable, which is a gentle, friendly, *Hi, here I am*. This was a concerned—you might say guilty—greeting. He was worried about me. And well might he be, the bastard!

It had started to rain and the mud was turning to red rivers, running down my face and my clothes. Somehow I managed to get the saddle off and him onto the trailer, and the tailgate lifted. There was no alternative—I had to do it.

He'd cracked a rib, of course, bashing me in the back with his shoulder and knocking me over. I was lucky he didn't stand right on me, but just on the edge of one calf, where I had an almighty bruise for weeks.

The accident was just an accident—one of those freak things that sometimes happen if you spend a lot of time with horses. But his behaviour afterwards was interesting. I think that what he was showing was regret and concern: empathy. I'll never forget it. Empathy is one of the requirements for a moral sense, and that day I know he was feeling for me.

*

There are numerous stories of cross-species empathy and cooperation, including stories of humans being helped by animals: a gorilla picking up a child, dolphins protecting swimmers from a shark, and so on. Despite this, the idea of morality in animals probably seems absurd to most people. At best, animals might be considered on par with very young children, not yet capable of making moral decisions. But what are the elements that make up morality? Empathy, fairness and justice, cooperation, reciprocity, altruism. Some of these at least have been shown to exist among some species. In our human-centric view of the world, we've tended to see primates at the top of the animal tree, with other mammals below them. The assumption has often been that if an ape is not capable of a certain thing, then no other species will be. We are always looking for what is closest to *us*. But that doesn't necessarily tell us much about the animals.

In their groundbreaking book on animal morality *Wild Justice: The Moral Lives of Animals*, ethologist Marc Bekoff and philosopher Jessica Pierce started from this point: 'Looking for "precursors" of *human* morality, though interesting, is not the same as looking for moral behaviour in animals.'[47] If morality is exclusive to mammals, what about birds? What about the parrot Alex? How to explain his complex array of behaviours and emotions; his humour and *contrition*. If morality is a kind of social intelligence that utilises a variety of skills, capacities and experiences, then he displayed that. And so do many other animals.

According to Bekoff and Pierce, moral behaviour is present in a large number of species. It has been found so far in chimps, wolves, elephants and rats. And there has only been limited research so far. Whales and dolphins are certainly candidates. Two of the more poignant experiments involved a pair of rats and a pair of mice. In one experiment, with rats, the rat had to push a lever for food but every time it did so, the rat in the adjoining cage received an electric shock. As soon as it realised that, the first rat refused to push the lever. Similar studies have been done, with chimps, other animals and birds, with similar results.

In an accidental experiment, two mice were trapped in a sink that they couldn't climb out of. They were not discovered for some time. One of the mice had become very weak and wouldn't move. Some food and water were put into the sink and the stronger mouse coaxed the weak one towards the water by holding a titbit of food in front of it, and gradually moving the food closer to the water. If moral behaviour is empathising with others, behaving fairly, being a moral *agent*, surely this mouse displayed it?

Assuming that humans have morality and that animals don't may be nothing more than a habit of mind. One more denial of who animals are, and that they, too, can display fairness, reciprocity and empathy. According to Bekoff and Pierce, the threshold requirements for morality are:

- a level of complexity in social organisation

- norms of behaviour that distinguish right and wrong

- a level of neural complexity that serves as a foundation for decision-making based on perceptions of the past and the future

- relatively advanced cognitive capacities (e.g. a good memory)

- a high level of behavioural flexibility.

Domestic animals are not included in the list of animals so far tested for moral behaviour, but most tick these boxes. Many animal behaviourists would still doubt the capacity for perceiving the past and the future in a range of animals, horses included. Andrew McLean's experiments, for example, cast strong doubt on the ability of horses to 'remember' in an abstract way. But horses do remember the things they are afraid of; people and situations that frighten them.

I have no way of knowing for certain why Vincent whinnied at me in that concerned way that day. It could have been that it had nothing to do with him knocking me over—he may have already 'forgotten' the incident a few minutes before. It could be that he was merely responding to the distress he could see and feel in me. That is quite likely. I am not suggesting that he was actually feeling guilty. But he was certainly aware that I was suffering and it made him anxious *for me*. That was the remarkable thing. I've seen him anxious about himself many times but this was something entirely different. He was standing quite still, watching me. When he is feeling anxious himself he is invariably restless, moving around a lot, doing 'anxious poos', shaking his head. But there was none of that.

I do believe that horses are one of those animals that are extraordinarily good at reading humans. They can instantly pick up what is 'right' or 'wrong', in human terms, from the human who is with them. In their own social group there are also rituals about the right or wrong way to behave.

Among animals, as among humans, morality is a way of maintaining social order. The rituals and customs that individuals of many species display among themselves are to that end. Being able to 'read' a situation is essential to them. The harm or benefit of certain actions are a moral currency, part of negotiating a life's path. While competition for food and sexual favours have long been seen as dominant reasons for why animals act the way they do, it ignores the very many instances of animal cooperation, sometimes with the same end in mind, but sometimes for other reasons. Sometimes animals will cooperate for the good of the group, other times because of an individual who is ill. It is quite common for a group of animals to stay with one of their number who is ill, or to moderate their pace to that of the slowest member.

This has been seen often with elephants. Elephants are also known to perform a death ritual for a dead elephant. They gather round and scream, then touch the body quietly with their trunks, then throw branches and dirt over the body. They stay with the body, their trunks hanging limply, sometimes for days. Or go away for food and water, then return.

Such rituals have been seen to occur even when the dead elephant was a stranger to the group. Remarkably, elephants have appeared to mourn a human. When African conservationist Lawrence Anthony, known as the Elephant Whisperer, died in 2012, a herd of elephants, who had not been spotted for some time, came to the conservationist's house on his reserve.

They also show great interest in the remains of previously buried elephants, sometimes sorting the bones with their trunks. It is well known that elephants grieve. What is less well known is the enormous loss and dysfunction in elephant societies. A hundred years ago there were 10 million wild elephants; now there are about 400,000. This has led to a loss of matriarchs, the leaders of the herds, and a loss of caring role models as well as an increase in dysfunctional and dangerous young males. In other words, social breakdown.

Bekoff and Pierce again: 'When human societies disintegrate and the social fabric becomes damaged, people often lose their moral bearings. This may be equally true for animal societies held together by normative standards of behaviour. This suggests, among other things, that in planning for conservation, we need to pay particular attention to conserving intact and functioning societies, not just saving individual animals.'[48] This suggests that there may be an ancient layer of moral behaviour that humans share with animals: empathy (sympathy, compassion, grief, consolation), cooperation (altruism, reciprocity, honesty, trust) and justice (sharing, equity, fair play, forgiveness).

Bekoff and Pierce have been accused of simplifying the idea of morality to make it fit with animals. But they argue that 'giving a broad description that encompasses its diversity and range is going to give it more meaning, not less'.[49]

While the old nature-or-nurture argument is now considered overly simplistic, and it is recognised that behaviour is a complex interplay of factors, it is still true that moral behaviour is linked to biology, to genes and neurons. Given that there is a good deal of similarity between the biology of humans and other mammals, it should not be surprising if some of the moral hardwiring is similar.

The functioning of mirror neurons is said to be one of the most important discoveries in neuroscience in recent years. These are neurons that fire in response to the execution and observation of behaviours. They do so not only when an animal carries out an action—such as a monkey grabbing an apple out of a box—but when it sees the same action performed by another. Mirror neurons are thought to play a role in empathy. Just how important they are is contentious.[50] It is believed they are what allows an individual to 'copy' another, and also to intuit the feelings of others. Research into mirror neurons is still at an early stage; so far they have been found in monkeys, humans, some birds and probably dogs.

Spindle cells are another part of the neurological puzzle which may throw light on emotions. Spindle cells are the linkages that allow rapid emotional judgements. They are also what allow for self-recognition and self-consciousness. They certainly exist in primates and whales and probably in other animals. Whales have been found to have three times as many spindle cells as humans.

Such neurological discoveries bolster the evidence provided by the animals themselves, through their observed behaviour. Experiments on empathy in animals are often incredibly cruel. And the stress levels of experimental animals often compromise the data. There is a need for a different way of studying such things. Observation, anecdote and narrative may not have the acceptability of scientific 'evidence' but can provide many clues, and may even be more useful in requiring us to remove the blinkers and prejudices and really *look*.

When the two mice were trapped in the sink, the human who discovered them displayed sympathy, by providing food and water; the stronger mouse demonstrated both empathy and sympathy, encouraging the sick mouse to take refreshments and nourishment—putting herself out to be of assistance.

If animals have the capacity for empathy, they have a basic building block for what we call morality. Empathy isn't a single behaviour but it shows an emotional link. Sometimes it can be demonstrated through body mimicry—copying what is seen. At other times what occurs is emotional contagion, when an animal takes on the feelings of one of its companions. One sees that all the time with horses, in how fearfulness can spread among them. This is an almost automatic physiological response. Then there is cognitive empathy—the ability to feel another individual's emotion and understand the reasons for it. So did Vincent understand what had happened when he knocked me over, or did he simply pick up on my distress, as in an emotional contagion?

In humans, empathy is not mediated by conscious thought: it is a response, pure interaction. By reading another person's expressions we have a fair idea of what they are experiencing. It does not require cognition. Therefore animals, which may be less cognitive than we are, may be just as capable of empathy.

*

The lives of animals are not shaped just by competition and conflict. It is only part of their story, as it is part of ours. This seems so self-evident, such common sense, yet it is a radical idea to animal researchers with closed minds about animal intelligence.

Cooperation for the good of the group has not been given sufficient credence because it seems to contradict the idea of animals competing for individual survival. But animals cooperate far more than they have conflict.

Mutual grooming, which is often seen in apes in particular, is a sign of mutual aid. The apes are often looking for and removing parasites on their friend. We have seen something similar in action in two older dogs we have recently taken on the care of. The female, Ginger, is a big ridgeback/Labrador cross; the male, Bodhi, a cattle dog cross. They have been together all their lives. When he was younger, Bodhi suffered from a skin condition caused by an allergy to a particular kind of grass. Ginger got into the habit of grooming him, licking and nuzzling the sore bits of skin. It must have been a great relief and comfort to Bodhi because when she does it now, he gets a blissed-out expression on his face. He no longer suffers from the allergy but the habit of grooming has been maintained between them. Bodhi never grooms Ginger—it is always the other way around. It may be that she developed the habit in part from a frustrated mothering impulse. She is certainly the dominant one of the two.

Among animals, as among humans, behaviour becomes immoral when it violates an established norm. What those 'norms' may be varies between different kinds of animals. So morality is species-dependent; each species must be evaluated on its own terms. Different species display cooperation and reciprocity, for example, in different ways. Yet can we then say, as Bekoff and Pierce do, that 'Empathy and cruelty both rely on the ability to imagine how one's own behaviour affects others'?[51] Does that really follow?

Isn't that an example of trying to apply a human conceptualisation to animals?

*

Some researchers say that animals do not have the necessary mechanism to partake in reciprocal altruism, another kind of moral behaviour. That the requirements – counting, learning, memory, the ability to estimate time, the use of reputation for assessing potential partners – are lacking in animals. But I would say that many domestic animals have some or all of these to some degree. Whether they use them to display reciprocal altruism is another matter.

If a dog is accustomed to receiving three treats after dinner and you only offer two, then he knows and will wait for the third. If you then produce a fourth he will have already turned away and will look back at you, surprised, thus demonstrating counting, learning and memory. A dog also knows when it is time for a walk or the time of day when their master usually comes home. They may not measure time as we do, but they recognise the passing of the day. As for using reputation to assess potential friends or partners, this we may never know. But we can observe animals assessing one another and making judgements, then teaming up or avoiding one another. Evidence of this can be found in any dog park.

Humans have different kinds of intelligence: linguistic, spatial, logical. Animals, too, have different kinds of intelligence and the list will look different for each species. When Andrew McLean says horses are not very intelligent he is saying that they don't think like us, and he is saying it because he doesn't want people to think they can talk to their horse as if it is human and expect it to understand, and then get annoyed when it doesn't.

With animals—perhaps with all of us—there are links between sociality and intelligence. Cats are considered solitary creatures but in fact are extremely interested in other cats, in particular in their smells, which transmit information. This, to a cat, is a social interaction. They don't necessarily have to be with the other cat.

Bekoff and Pierce state, 'Animals need brains that can tie together past and present and make good guesses about the future. They also need brains that can make reasonably accurate assessments about intentions and emotional states of other animals, both friends and strangers. They must be able to anticipate the behaviour of a social partner, which involves "mentalising"—attributing independent mental states to others, seeing them as distinct social actors with thoughts and emotions different from the animal's own. Animals must also possess considerable behavioural flexibility, such as being able to choose or suppress a certain course of action, based on an assessment of its likely outcomes.'[52] This suggests that animals think, and that they make judgements, including moral judgements. But scientific understanding of social cognition in animals is still very limited.

The kind of social evaluation that humans do even as babies, animals probably do, too. And these kinds of evaluation are the building blocks of notions such as justice and fairness. Animals show through their behaviour their reactions to fairness or injustice, such things as pleasure, indignation, trust, forgiveness, retribution. These things are not hard for a human to identify when observing a group of animals. When animals play, they show pleasure but they also demonstrate fairness—play is all about fairness. There might be mock aggression, but it is mock.

When a dog wants to play, it makes the play bow, lowering itself to the other dog, asking to play. An older animal can often be seen downplaying its strength when playing with a younger animal. Younger animals learn the rules through play: how hard can I bite, how rough can I be. They also learn to resolve conflicts and misunderstandings.

Play can inspire joy in one's companions. Cats, dogs, horses, bears—when one animal is feeling good and starts to play, the others become infected with joy. Unlike humans, who have established a complex set of abstract principles around justice and injustice, animals likely experience these things as a feeling. Much as we can *feel* hard done by.

The Dutch ethologist Frans de Waal believed animals had empathy but thought that morality required making a judgement about something external, and they probably could not do that. To him, human morality was still unique, more nuanced. But he recognised that animals may well still have a sense of fairness. He observed that when all members of a group of monkeys were fed cucumbers, harmony ensued. But if one monkey was given grapes—a food monkeys prefer to cucumbers—the others protested by rattling their cages and throwing away their cucumbers.[53]

When Lina has to be kept locked up, because of her sore foot or because she is too fat, she certainly feels the unfairness of it. And she makes her displeasure known! That ear-splitting hee-haw.

If animals can't be impartial, well, impartiality is only important in some forms of justice. Fairness is rather different in that it involves a capacity to compare. Animals may lack reflective self-control but such reflective judgement is not necessarily essential for moral behaviour. Many of our own moral actions happen without it. Animals monitor one another's behaviour, and it may be this that leads at times to demonstrably moral action.

I have just eaten a biscuit with my coffee. Ginger and Bodhi sit beside my desk watching me with great concentration. They watch my hands, my mouth. They can't believe it—I have eaten the entire biscuit and have not given them *any*! Is this fair! Is this justice!

Chapter 18
No Expectations

I sit on the grass near where Lina is standing. I have my back to her as I gaze down the hill to where the horses are grazing. She walks over to me, silent on her delicate hooves. I feel her presence behind me. She begins by rubbing her nose on my back, between my shoulder blades. I can just imagine the green stains I am getting on my shirt. I lean back a little towards her and she increases her pressure against me. She rubs her forehead a few times against my spine then nuzzles the back of my shoulder. We lean towards each other and she begins messing with my hair. I feel her breath in my ear. Will she bite my ear, or pull out a lump of my hair? Not likely; we're having a mutual love-in. I turn my head slightly towards her and she rubs her muzzle against my cheek. Which is softer: her muzzle or my cheek?

She is a small animal but nonetheless I am on the ground and further down the hill, so at a disadvantage. It is a potentially vulnerable situation. I reach around and scratch her between her front legs, where the hair is short and smoothest. She likes this; this is something new. Finally I stand up and she leans her face into my chest in her usual way, while I rub her long ears, one ear in each of my hands.

I have shown my trust in her and she shows hers in me. With Lina there is no battle of wills and no expectation. We simply enjoy each other's company. The only time there is discord between us is if I want her to go somewhere she doesn't want to, that is, when I set up an expectation – expecting her to comply. Then there can be a brief battle of wills, although these days it is usually just a game.

It is those relationships with animals that do not involve expectation that seem to be the most successful. As soon as human expectation enters the equation the relationship can go awry. I have seen it in dogs, and particularly in horses. Because we tend to expect that they will behave in a way that makes sense to us humans—but may make no sense to them.

To some trainers, this means working without expectations. The 'being with' is the crucial thing. A bond develops and, ultimately, the animal will cooperate *because it wants to*. Trying to subdue expectations is a very difficult thing. And perhaps even impossible, because surely even the most non-dogmatic animal trainer has a plan, or a hope, as to how they would like the animal to behave? But if the bond is strong enough, it appears that the animal learns through mirroring the trainer. The wanting to please can be a powerful motivator.

Trust and acceptance, and the recognition that that is a two-way process, is central to such a theory of animal behaviour and training.

This is in marked contrast to 'learning theory' as it is applied to animals, which is basically a reward system. You do what I want, you get a reward. Sometimes the reward is food but with horses it is usually just the release of pressure. At its most basic level: I pull on the reins, you stop. You stop, I stop pulling on the reins.

In their purest form, these are two very different schools of thought. But most people who own or train animals are probably muddling around somewhere in between. On the one hand, trying to establish a rapport with an animal, hoping to reach a point where it seems to know what you want almost without you doing anything. And when that fails or is only partially successful, resorting to a pressure and reward system.

Trusting the animal is one thing; trusting oneself is another – and is probably more important. A confident person exudes that and animals can sense it. The best relationships we can have with animals occur when the animal accepts us and is prepared to concede leadership to us.

*

My friend Vicki has bought a muzzle to put on her mare to stop her from eating so much. I was a bit alarmed when I heard. I suggested the mare might be very frustrated by the muzzle and how about just locking her up overnight in a small paddock or yard, with one of the other horses for company? But Vicki said she was only leaving the muzzle on for short periods at the moment, and that the mare could still pick the odd leaf of grass through it and that so far she was accepting it very sweetly. And that at least she could move around the paddock and wasn't standing still for long periods.

Vicki is heading down the path that is generically known as 'natural horsemanship' (NH), although there are many variations on that theme. This is a range of methods guided by kindness and empathy, that reject coercive methods of horse training. She is serious-minded in her pursuit of a better way to handle and care for horses, reading and talking widely, and going on courses. She has moved a long way from the confines of the Dutch riding school where she learnt to ride. There are a lot of things that she won't do any more, like stable a horse. We have to agree to disagree quite often. But we keep talking, and it's interesting. The divergence in our thinking is emblematic of the wider horse world, where proponents of natural horsemanship tend to see 'traditional' methods as anathema, and the traditionalists see the NH practitioners as woolly headed devotees. A lot of NH people, indeed, tend to behave as if they have 'found God', expounding their views with incredible vehemence. They also, like a lot of people who get caught up in New Age theories, frequently jump from one guru to another.

I don't feel comfortable in either camp. The divisions between the traditionalists and the NH practitioners are often portrayed as vast, and there are some extremists: at one end, people who want their horse to be a performance machine; at the other, those who want their horse to love them as they love their horse. But mostly the differences are exaggerated. The majority of performance riders love their horse (maybe not all of their horses, but there will be horses they have loved) and most NH adherents do actually want to be able to do something with their horse, like ride them, maybe even compete.

NH believers are extremely critical of performance riders (dressage, show jumping, eventing), citing harsh bits used to restrain and control, bullying of the horse, whips, spurs and excessive pressure. Yet very few high-performance riders will get very far, or be successful for long, with such tactics.

The fundamental issues are those of liberty and control. To what extent do we allow, even celebrate, the animal's natural freedom and to what extent do we attempt to control it? There is this dichotomy, particularly in the NH literature. Proponents of natural horsemanship want the horse to have liberty and to choose to cooperate with the human.

Many NH adherents speak in almost a romantic way about 'partnership' with the horse as their ultimate wish fulfilment. But this is at odds with their other desire, to let the horse be a horse. Working with the horse on the ground, with the horse at liberty, is seen as a pinnacle of cooperation. The human is asking for the horse to make certain moves and the horse is offering that behaviour willingly. Done well, it is a beautiful thing to watch. But the element of human control is still there—the horse is still doing what the human wants.

Natural horsemanship and all its many manifestations seem to appeal particularly to a new generation of riders and horse owners, primarily women, who want above all a good relationship with their horse. While the gurus are mostly male, their followers are mostly female. It started as an alternative movement but now is becoming more mainstream. I first became aware of it on the NSW Far North Coast—not surprising perhaps. Lots of 'alternatives' up there. Now there are scores of books and videos, workshops and trainers.

I've been a bit nonplussed by it. I think my relationship with my first horse, Beauty, was one of total harmony. She was an exceptional mare and when I was eight or nine I could do anything with her. Contact with the mouth was unnecessary; anything I wanted of her could be achieved with the lightest of weight and other aids. She was willing but not hot, quiet but not lazy.

At the weekend I judged some dressage at the local pony club and was reminded how irrelevant to young riders are notions of contact (in which the reins are stretched in a straight line between the horse's mouth and rider's hands) and collection (when a horse's centre of gravity is shifted backwards to allow a horse to move more athletically). The eight and nine year olds were happy if their ponies trotted when they were supposed to and cantered when they were supposed to and did roughly circular circles. Those who had 'contact' were the ones who were hanging on to the horse's mouth to make it stay roughly on track.

The natural horsemanship adherents want their horses to go in beautiful self-carriage, collection even, but without any contact with the horse's mouth. It may be possible to teach a horse to do this, but most people are only going to succeed when the horse they are working with has the temperament and paces and natural ability to carry itself in 'self-carriage'. Collection is the ultimate, very often unobtainable, goal in a dressage horse, when it carries itself in a light and compact frame and is responsive to the lightest touch from the rider. But NH people want more than this. They want a horse that relates to them—that will follow them around, that wants to be with them. Maybe it is very gratifying to the ego.

I must admit, Vincent doesn't do this. He ignores me, far more than old Jim. If you are around, Jim is keen to talk to you. But Vincent, on the whole, has other things on his mind. Yesterday I tried just being with him, to see if he would focus on me. I sat a few metres away from him and waited for him to turn towards me. He didn't but kept gazing out at that damned view of his. Eventually I produced a carrot—that got his attention.

But I realised that while waiting for him to look at me I had basically been setting him a test. And I realised that that is what I do with him, often. I am always setting him tests and he just doesn't want that from me. It is probably the source of the difficulties between us.

OK, from now on, no tests. Games then? But what is the difference between a test and a game? Really, he likes it when I am just with him and not expecting anything of him. That is hard, although it shouldn't be.

To expect nothing. Very Buddhist.

*

It was Vicki who introduced me to the work of Marta Williams and of Klaus Hempfling. She has been my window into that world. Both Williams and Hempfling have extraordinary talent: Marta to intuit what is going on with an animal; and Klaus in showing people how to make a deep connection with a horse. The fascination here is with the human–animal bond. Williams believes that if we 're-find' our intuitive connection with animals, we can actually 'talk' to them. That we can find out about their lives by intuiting information from them.

A la Marta, I've been talking to the animals a lot more lately, to see if it changes anything between us. I do think they like the focused attention. She says one should practise on friends' animals but I don't see the point in that as it is mine that I want to know about. The first time I tried talking to Vincent I sat down with him in his stable to ask him some serious questions, but I quite clearly got the message that he wasn't interested in talking; he was far more interested in getting out to the paddock.

I have had a bit more success since and I notice that he is a lot less standoffish, really wanting his ears scratched. I asked him about going to my friend Sally's up north again this year. I got the feeling he is not all that keen, although I suspect he can be talked around with promises of going to the beach!

I asked the cat, Charlie, if he would mind if we got a new dog. He was nervous and not happy about that, but not completely freaked either. Again, I suspect he can be talked around. Or am I, in both cases, just hoping they will accept what I have already decided?

Regardless of whether there is anything really in this 'conversation' idea, I do think that focusing on the animal, talking to it, and even negotiating with it, is likely to lead to a more harmonious relationship. I have real doubts about them understanding the actual words but I do feel they sense something of what I am on about. I've always talked to all my animals but in a fairly automatic, offhand way. This giving them focused attention as I do it, thinking of them as truly sentient beings as I talk to them, takes things to another level. Once you start doing it you become more fully aware that this animal is or can be a friend, that you live in proximity and that they should be treated as a member of the family. We often say that of pets but how often do we really 'discuss' things with them as we would with another member of the family? Yet, by doing so, it emphasises to us their interconnectedness with us.

Lately I've been thinking about my connection and confidence with horses; the intuitive *feel* that I had as a child rider. Since I've gone back to riding more seriously, trying to train Vincent to be a dressage horse, I've found it is not as easy as it used to be when I was a child. My timing in those days was fantastic. I could ask for an aid at precisely the right moment to get what I wanted (something I now find much more difficult). When I was showjumping I always counted down the last three strides and was able to make the horse adjust the length of its stride so that it arrived in front of the fence in exactly the right place for take-off. If I got those three strides right, everything else followed, and I almost always did. I used to think that I was able to do it because I have a good spatial sense, for distances in particular, so I knew when to start counting 1, 2, 3. But I think there was more to it than that: the horse and I were counting those last three strides together.

Chapter 19
The Healing Power of Animals

The healing power of horses has a long history. The ancient Greek physician Hippocrates, considered the father of medicine, wrote about the therapeutic potential of horseback riding more than 2000 years ago. More recently, equine therapy has been used to benefit a range of physical and mental health issues, from substance abuse and traumatic brain injury to eating disorders and dementia.

Groundbreaking work in Western Australia's remote Kimberley has brought horses and Indigenous youths together for the first time to improve mental health, in a region with some of the world's highest rates of youth suicide. Devised and run by Indigenous researcher Professor Juli Coffin, the Broome-based Yawardani Jan-ga / Helping Horses initiative assists young people, aged six to twenty-six, to build confidence and awareness, and regulate their emotions through interacting with horses. Coffin believes horses have particular qualities that can make for a therapeutic interaction.

'They're non-judgmental, they don't care what you did yesterday or what you are going to do tomorrow. And they are very reflective... They also offer this beautiful non-verbal communication,' Coffin told ABC Radio. 'Also [horses] model for us really good relationships in their herd environment so that if they have an altercation, for example, they go back to grazing, you know? Two seconds later, they're back eating together and they have a nice structure...some young people have never had that.'[54]

This world-first program, for which Coffin was honoured in the 2021 WA Mental Health Awards, is already having benefits. With improved life skills and the ability to regulate emotions as a result of interacting with the horses, young students are already performing better in school.

It is not only the healing power of horses that has been harnessed in recent years. A range of animals have been used, from dolphins and fish to guinea pigs and ferrets, but especially dogs. No longer used primarily as companions for the visually impaired, dogs are now making their presence felt everywhere—in the courts and theatres, and even at the Sydney Opera House.

Aged-care homes used to be pet-free zones. Residents not only had to relinquish their much-loved pets before they entered, often the animals were not even allowed to visit their former owners. Mercifully, that is now changing. Many facilities welcome animals. Visitors are encouraged to bring the family pet, most commonly dogs, and some aged-care homes have specially trained canine visitors. Anyone who has worked in or visited such a facility will have seen elderly faces light up when a pooch appears for a pat. Research suggests that the presence of pets in aged care can help reduce blood pressure, confusion and fatigue, and aid a range of physical and psychological problems in elderly people.[55]

Even the presence of an artificial dog can improve mental health. In one study, a group of nursing home residents had weekly thirty-minute visits from Sparky, a real dog, while others were visited by Aibo, a doggie robot. A control group received no visits. Sparky and Aibo spent time in residents' rooms, each wagged their tail and responded to the people they visited. After seven weeks, residents were asked about how lonely they felt. The most surprising finding was that those who received visits from either the real or robotic dog felt less lonely than the group who didn't receive any visits. It made no difference whether the dog was real or battery-operated.[56]

Dogs are also increasingly being used in prisons, including under an innovative scheme in Queensland that puts prisoners and puppies together. Under the scheme an inmate is assigned a puppy and will care for it twenty-four hours a day for up to two years. The goal is that the puppy will then become an assistance dog for a person living with a disability.

The program helps with an ongoing challenge: the demand for assistance dogs outstrips the ability to find volunteers willing to give the time and energy to train a puppy. But it has also had benefits for inmates. A study of the ten-year program found prisoners had a 94 per cent increase in overall wellbeing, a 32 per cent improvement in confidence and self-esteem, and a 25 per cent improvement in mental wellness.[57]

In a Californian scheme, dogs at high risk of being euthanised have been rescued from animal shelters and paired with inmates. The goal is to train the dogs so they can become sufficiently socialised to eventually find a forever home with a member of the public. Inmates report beneficial effects from the program, including learning how to trust, to take responsibility and gain self-respect. In addition, of seventeen participants who afterwards received parole, none had returned to prison. This is significant in a prison system where recidivism rates are more than 40 per cent.[58]

*

It is a glorious autumn morning—sunny, with no wind. It will probably get to 16 or 17 degrees. I took Vincent out for a ride as it was just too nice to think about working in the arena. He is always a little nervous when out on his own, looking sideways at the most innocuous things. Then something truly scary comes along, like the great big gas tanker in the lane this morning, and he walks past calmly. He is so good at opening and shutting gates, too. Because he is so tall, I often have to lean right out of the saddle to reach down to the catch, and generally he stands like a rock. Today something frightened him while I was opening a gate—a big bird, I think. He bunched, quivered all over, but didn't swing away, as if he knew he mustn't do anything that would lead me to fall off.

Coming back through the neighbours' front paddocks, a lovely series of rolling hills, I could tell he was dying to have a run but we walked, because he might well have tried something naughty there. When we got back to our place I allowed him a gentle canter and he was calm and relaxed, didn't even try to rush.

Working with Vincent on the ground is changing things between us. He enjoys it and so do I. We started with simple things: getting him to walk on a loose lead, keeping a good distance between us, and not getting ahead of me. Stopping immediately when I stop—I raised my hand and initially held the long whip up in front of him. He learnt that one quickly. Then trotting, with the lead loose and him staying the same distance from me. Walk, trot, halt, walk, trot, walk, halt, trot, walk. That kind of thing. He began to watch me, not looking around or over the fence, but concentrating on me.

Once he got used to this, I unclipped the lead and just looped it loosely around his neck, then did the same thing. Now he will do the walk, trot, halt without any lead at all, and move around the arena keeping roughly level with me. Yesterday we started figures of eight, with him changing direction through the circle as I move my body. I need to refine my movements because it is easy to confuse him. One of the ways I can tell he is getting the message is that now, when we trot and I run beside him, he will alter his pace to keep in position beside me—slow, fast, slow.

It only requires ten or fifteen minutes of this kind of work a day. I feel pleased with him and get the definite impression he feels he has achieved something. He doesn't behave as if it's a chore that he is keen to finish, but rather something that we do together. I feel we're closer than we were, more in harmony.

I've struggled with Vincent for a long time, trying, I now realise, to make him into something he isn't; trying to make him fit some conception of mine. Dressage is a difficult discipline. It can be quite intellectual in a way—there are many theories, about the horse, how it learns, moves, what feels comfortable to it, what is easy, what is hard. I've read and thought about it a lot, for years now. In fact, I've thought about it too much. I'm no longer listening to my instincts, my body, my horse. Always trying *for* something, and being disappointed.

The struggle has made both Vincent and me unhappy. Unhappy with each other. Is it any wonder that he often doesn't seem very pleased to see me? I've felt almost jealous at times at how easily my sister Jenny seems to get on with him when she rides him. Because she thinks he is gorgeous and good. And he knows it.

'The work' became an enormous boulder between Vincent and me. One that I placed there. And yet he is so forgiving! A few unstressful encounters, a few days where I petted him but asked nothing of him, and he's fond again.

I've known for some time that a large part of the problem is my expectations. I've tried to put those aside, to be relaxed and undemanding when I ride. But that has only worked to a point. Indeed, sometimes it has been counterproductive: I've become so passive that poor Vincent is lost, confused. *Where is she? Where is my leader?* I see now what has been missing: joy and appreciation. Or appreciation and joy. Because when I appreciate dear Vincent for what he is—his beauty and floating gaits, his lightness and erect carriage and willingness—it makes me joyful and he feels my joy and is happy in turn. He is so attuned to my frame of mind! More so, I suspect, than any animal I've known—even, perhaps, more than my dogs, famous for their attentiveness to one's emotions.

I have said to Vincent: 'You don't have to be a dressage horse; just be yourself'. And how happy that has made him, and me! He has stopped fidgeting when I saddle him up, and shying at invisible things in the arena, and chomping on his bit. He enjoys being with me again.

This morning, after I had ridden him, I groomed him and he was totally relaxed. I took his head-collar off to brush his face. He did not attempt to move away but lowered his head so it was an inch from my chest and luxuriated in every brush stroke, turning his head on its side slightly so I could get to the itchy bit under his throat. This is the side of him that I've been missing…oh, for a long time now. The anxiety between us has fallen away and we are friends again.

I've learnt an important lesson, one that I must have known when I was a kid but had forgotten. To listen to my horse. To be myself and let him be himself. To stop working for some weird 'ideal' and enjoy what we have. I've been too dependent on the advice of others—reading books, a string of coaches. Maybe I did learn a lot but I also forgot a lot. And maybe the things I forgot were more important.

Chapter 20
Life and Death

It's September, and the time for calving. The rhododendrons are flowering and the bulbs have been good this year—a result of good rains after they flowered last year—but it has been a very dry winter and there is little green feed for the cows and their offspring.

The first cow to calve was a shock. Having given no sign that a birth was imminent, there were suddenly two small brown bodies on the ground early one morning. She'd had twins, and only one was alive. As well, her womb had prolapsed. It was touch and go for the little survivor. But with handfeeding he began to improve. Now, five days later, he can get up and totter around after his mother and he's beginning to get the hang of drinking from her. And she, too, is recovering from the ordeal.

Yesterday another cow calved, and this time it was trouble-free, the calf up and drinking, and gambolling about his mother within hours. Again, this cow gave no real indication that she was about to calve.

One-Eye, on the other hand, has been looking huge for weeks, and her udder has been full for at least a week. The teats were so engorged that they stuck out to the side. We've been worried about her because she lost her calf last year—it was born dead, or maybe died during the birth. I found it half in, half out of poor One-Eye. This year we wanted to make sure the same thing didn't happen again. So Jan and I were up at the cow paddock at six and One-Eye was clearly beginning to be in labour. Two hours later she was straining and some liquid emerged. Then she seemed to stop trying. We got the vet out, and it was a good thing we did because the calf was in the wrong position—hind feet first rather than front feet first. And it was a big, big calf. Ken, the vet, felt around inside and got a rope around the calf's legs, then he positioned the calving pole, which has a curved bar that sits against the cow's haunches, and a winch on the long handle to winch the calf out. Slowly this enormous heifer emerged. It was covered in the birth sack and stained yellow. The yellow staining was from the calf's first manure, and a sign that it had been under stress for some time. I was very nervous about whether she would be alive or not. Calving might be a natural thing for a cow to do. But *farming* calves like this suddenly felt wrong.

But she was alive! And what a whopper of a calf! One-Eye would have had no chance of delivering her on her own. A few more hours and the calf would have been dead, and the cow might not have been too good either. Left alone both might have died. Is this the bargain we strike: to exploit but also care for them?

We let the cow out of the cattle crush and she went straight to where we had lain the calf and began to lick her clean. Unlike the little surviving twin, this big heifer was trying to get to her feet within minutes. In between licking the calf, One-Eye had a big drink of water and when I later gave her half a bucket of grain she ate greedily. She deserved it!

Four more calves to go, and I think they might be our last. There are three cows now who will be retired: Freckle, One-Eye and the mother of the twins. A retirement home for cows begins to sound like a very good idea.

*

The surviving calf from the twins has had a very mixed month. After appearing to be coming along quite well, he started plateauing, then going backwards.

September was unusually warm, but hardly had October begun when the weather changed and it was like winter again. Rain, sleet even, and bitter winds. Jan found the little fellow half frozen early one morning, so we took him back to the small cow shed where he had spent his first days and bedded him down in straw and rubbed him dry. His mum followed him into the shed and settled down beside him for the day, as if she, too, was glad to be out of the weather.

He has spent ten days in the shed, each day finding it seemingly harder to get up to drink. And he can't stand. He is getting much heavier, and it is becoming more difficult to get him up on his feet. The cow has found a solution to that. Yesterday morning she stood right over the top of him so he could drink from her without getting up. But it confirmed what we knew; he must be paralysed. We have to put him down.

*

'You did everything you could,' Ken the vet said when he came.

As happens with animals, the syringe was hardly empty before the calf was gone, lying in Jan's arms.

After a few moments we all moved back to allow the cow to come up to him.

'She'll need to see what's happened,' Ken said. 'It's best.'

She approached, still lowing softly, and stood and looked down at him. So tame she has become since he has been ill, letting us guide her and stroke her. We talked among ourselves as she looked down at her dead calf. Did she understand that he was dead? Could she sense it? Could she process it—or did she just feel it?

The other cows had moved away up the hill, grazing as they went. And once the dead calf was on the truck, his mother followed them. She didn't stop or look back.

But later in the afternoon, at the time when she would normally have come to him, to feed him, she came back to the spot where he had last lain. She stood and looked at that spot and mooed. And when she saw us nearby she looked at us and mooed. *Where is he? Produce him so I can feed him.*

We spoke to her, explained to her, told her that nothing more could be done for him, that it was for the best. She watched us as if listening. Then continued to just stand there, looking at that spot, mooing off and on; stopping for a while, then starting again.

All night it went on.

A cow loses many children in her lifetime, one after the other they are taken from her. But she is accustomed to feeding her baby until it can feed itself. For this cow, that purpose had suddenly been truncated. So she called and called; maybe not grief as a human mother would experience it, but grief for a natural order disrupted.

Death is often at one's elbow on a farm, and I find myself hovering on that uneasy terrain between hard-headedness and sentimentality. Few occupations confront one so intimately, and so often, with the tragic sweep of life.

*

Susan and I came home yesterday after a week away and immediately went for a walk around the farm. Charlie insisted on coming, too. I had to pick him up a few times because he gets left behind and complains.

I carried him into the front paddock where the weaners are and he and they seemed unconcerned by each other. They didn't take much notice of him while he was in my arms. However, when we moved back to the gate and I put him down outside they immediately became fascinated by him. They all rushed up to the fence to stare at him, and as we moved along the track parallel to the fence they followed us, or rather Charlie, some of them trotting and bucking in excitement. They only had eyes for the cat. He was understandably a bit intimidated by this but seemed to realise they couldn't get to him. So he followed us along the track, stopping and crouching and looking at the calves every few metres. They looked very cute—the seven of them in a line hard up against the fence, their heads lowered, staring in great fascination.

We didn't manage to get all around the farm. We gave up and picked Charlie up and turned back.

*

My sister Jen has more time now they've sold the restaurant and she wants to get back into riding. She spent more than a decade as a professional rider and trainer. But now she just wants to enjoy riding and has no great ambitions.

So I have gradually decided to give Vincent to Jenny. It's been hard because when I got him five years ago I thought we would have a partnership for life. And I've devoted an awful lot of love and time to him.

You develop an incredible bond with a horse, even if, or maybe even because, there are difficulties, miscommunications, unrealised expectations. Knowing what you want of the horse and knowing, theoretically, how to achieve it, is a very different thing from actually being able to make it happen when one is in the saddle. Vincent and I were very attuned to one another. The slightest tension in me manifested in him. The slightest anxiety in him made me anxious. We weren't good for one another. But I kept hoping. I'd invested a lot in the idea that we were a team and would stick together. It was hard to let go of that idea.

*

Vincent has gone. He'll come back, hopefully, sometimes, on holidays. But he and Jen are the team now. I hope he will be happy in his new home. He doesn't have a stable with the same wonderful view. I wonder if he'll miss it? And I wonder, when he does come home on holidays, if he'll go straight to his window and gaze out at his view, head high, white ears pricked, as if he had never been away.

Chapter 21
A New Farm, a Different Life

When one has only a few cows, one inevitably personalises them: we give them names, consider their individual personalities. And we've indulged ourselves in this. Indeed, we chose Herefords because slight differences in their white markings make it easier to tell them apart.

But all this may be about to change. We've talked for years about moving somewhere flatter, because the hilliness of this country makes it hard to get around, and therefore hard on the knees. We briefly flirted with going further west and getting a big property—some echoes from those childhood Mary Grant Bruce books set on the fictional Billabong outback cattle station must have been singing in our veins. But more recently we had come to assume that if we were to move, it would be to a small property. Being sensible. And sometimes we've thought that we could never move at all, because nothing could compare with the magic of our private valley.

Then we found Virginia Park. It is only ten minutes away—on the top of the plateau, rather than on the edge of the escarpment. So it is flatter, big open country, and 300 acres of it. That is big for around here.

There are long avenues of trees bordering many of the paddocks: eucalypts, but also conifers, claret ash, ornamental pears, alders. The driveway is lined with liquidambars. There is only a very small section of road frontage—a couple of hundred metres. Most of the property is tucked away, hidden from the outside world.

About two-thirds is level to gently sloping, but in the back corner is a steep wild valley. It is beautiful down there with thick grass in the valley and trees on the slopes, dense in parts. Some parts are very steep. When I walked the boundary, I had to get down on my hands and knees and crawl, it was so steep. After rain, little streams run across the grassy base of the valley.

We bought the place because we fell in love with it. It wasn't sensible. One of my first thoughts was that we would need a part-time manager to help look after it. I wasn't planning on doing much of the farming myself. But now I am intrigued by its potential. It's quite run-down. A lot of the fencing is poor or non-existent. The cattle yards are so old a lot of the rails are almost rotted through. One of the barns is almost falling down. And the pastures have had no care for years. The whole place needs renovation. It is a major project.

So now we are faced not with downsizing but with upscaling. And rather than keeping a retirement home for cows, it looks like we'll be breeding. If we improve the pastures it will carry 100 head with ease. We won't be able to name all those cows, nor would we want to. Because with the new property comes not only a lot of work but also a lot of questions. Susan is interested in what we might be able to do with the land but it is the beauty of it that most draws her. It is I who will be 'the farmer'.

It's been beef cattle country for a long time, although that could change. We could run sheep, set up a dairy, raise pigs, farm free-range poultry. Whatever animals we farm, the question will be 'how to do it well'.

That means giving them a good life, which means also a longer life than animals destined for the dinner table usually get. It means thinking about the land, and the potential for farming it without chemicals or fertilisers wherever possible.

It also means investigating local abattoirs, trying to make the animals' last journey as short and unstressful as possible, and local distribution networks, so as not to become party to the contagion of excess food miles.

The whole issue of food is becoming increasingly difficult. How did it happen that this most basic of human activities has become such a fraught moral and environmental problem? Nothing about it is simple for me at the moment. In part it is because of my growing squeamishness about eating flesh. But there is also the whole question of being a farmer, and what that means, and what it is okay to farm and what it is not okay to farm.

I could just run a few cattle, sit back and look at our wide acres and think 'how beautiful' and not worry too much about how productive they are. After all, there are a lot of 'farms' around here that don't produce all that much. But it feels wasteful. Particularly when the soils are good and the climate benign, and there are millions of people needing to be fed within a couple of hours drive.

So how to use the land well, and still keep it beautiful. That is the challenge. Especially for a novice farmer. So I read about dairies and raising pasture poultry and contemplate pig-rearing (while not eating pork). And probably I won't do any of these things because it is all too difficult.

And meanwhile, I forget to go to the farmers market, so the vegies we eat come from the supermarket. And I waste hours in front of the computer when I'd be better off outside, my hands in the soil.

In *The Omnivore's Dilemma*, Michael Pollan looks at food. How we farm it, kill it, gather it, cook it. This thing that should be so simple—eating—has become so problematic. In developed countries we are drowning in food, and yet obsessed with it. Witness the endless television cooking shows. Part of the problem for humans is that there are so many things that we can eat. The omnivore's dilemma. According to Pollan: 'Many anthropologists believe that the reason we evolved such big and intricate brains was precisely to help us deal with the omnivore's dilemma.'[59] And he posits, too, what some philosophers have suggested: that it is this omnivorousness which has led to the proliferation of ethical rules, manners and rituals around food. When you can eat anything it can be a free-for-all without some moral guidelines.

There were good, practical reasons for many of the customs humans developed around food. But there is another emerging issue for thinking omnivores. Just because you can eat anything, doesn't mean you should. Pollan argues that eating is political. How we eat determines the use we make of the world. Since World War II, an industrial revolution of the food chain has occurred whereby food production once totally reliant on the sun has been replaced with a system that draws much of its energy from fossil fuels.

The industrialisation of food production has obscured our relationships with the natural world. 'Forgetting, or not knowing in the first place, is what the industrial food chain is all about,' Pollan says, '...if we could see what lies on the far side of the increasingly high walls of our industrial agriculture, we would surely change the way we eat.'[60] And the amount of emotional and intellectual effort that goes into making decisions—at every single meal—about what to eat, when you really start thinking about it, means that it might just be simpler to say 'I don't eat meat' or 'I don't eat seafood'.

When it comes to eating animals, the choice seems to be between looking away (i.e. don't think about it) or becoming vegetarian. I certainly can no longer do the former. I'm becoming boring to have dinner with. Because someone has only got to say 'I only eat free-range chicken' and I'll start telling them what free-range really means. How the chickens are crammed into sheds when they are young and only when they are older given access to an outdoor run next to the shed—but by then they are so used to being inside they don't dare go out, and anyway they are killed a few weeks later. Or organic—how a steer producing 'organic beef' or a cow producing 'organic milk' might eat up their organic tucker in a feedlot and rarely see a pasture. If you think 'organic' means the animal lives a natural life, forget it. That is an outdated 'pastoral' view of organic. Organic, too, is now Big Business.

Pollan's book is about the American food system. Industrial farming there is far more intensive, and extensive, than in Australia. But we are heading in the same direction. It would be nice to think the forces pushing back against industrial farming—the 'free-range organic' (which starts to actually mean something), the local food movement, the pastured poultry or pastured pork, the awareness of what grass-fed rather than grain-fed actually *means*—might stop it in its tracks.

So to cattle. Good grasses keep carbon in the soil, so grazing cattle on thick and healthy and well-managed pasture is sustainable. A 500-kilo steer can feed a lot of people.

Pollan says that humans are, like other animals, meat eaters – that it is not 'a mere gastronomic preference'. Rather it is one of the things we share with animals. He says animal rightists want us to acknowledge all that we share with animals but at the same time deny one of the most basic commonalities.

It's true, too, that the species that humans have domesticated for their own use have thrived. It is when a species is no longer useful that they suffer and decline. No animal demonstrates that more clearly than the donkey. For a wide range of species, association with humans has benefited both. The bison became a successful herd animal because it was hunted by Native Americans. Forced to move about more, they kept the pastures in good health and able to support more of them. But what is good for a species is not the same as what is good for the individual animal.

*

Susan's little dog Sarah is not easy to understand. Although very small and fluffy, she is definitely not a lap dog. As with many dogs, it is not size that matters to her but personality, and she has plenty of that. The only time she seems to be conscious of her smallness is with very tall people. With them she has an unfortunate tendency to nip ankles, at least until she gets to know them.

Not long after buying Virginia Park, but before we moved here (when we were still building the house), Sarah disappeared.

We went out, leaving all three dogs in the garden. When we came home some hours later, only Ginger and Bodhi were waiting for us. We searched the paddocks, then further afield. We called friends, who then joined the search. We assumed she would turn up at dinnertime, but she didn't. We prayed that the next morning she would have miraculously reappeared, but she didn't. We rang the local radio station and they interviewed Susan, and the word spread. We began to get calls about sightings: 'opposite the railway station', 'I tried to catch her but she ran away', 'in Ringwood Lane—she wouldn't let me near her', 'on the main road'. Each time we would rush to the location but there'd be no sign of her. Another day passed. We were filled with dread. Such a little creature and out there crossing roads and railway lines.

On the third day, a call came: 'I think I've just seen your dog in Old Argyle Road'. That was miles away! Then Susan and I looked at each other: it was also on the way to Virginia Park...could she be heading there? She and the other dogs had been there quite a few times with us. But Sarah is too small to see out the car windows. How would she know how to get there? We rushed off to VP, as we called the new place, and split up. Susan looked for her around the driveway and the construction site that was the new house. I went out behind the barns, to the deserted cottage. I called her name. And suddenly there she was. Looking bedraggled, her long silky fur entangled with twigs and leaves and sticky grass seeds. The relief! Not just ours but hers, too.

Now Sarah is quite a celebrity in our area. The local paper wants to do a story about her—and for once she designed to sit on Susan's lap for the photograph. We worked out that she travelled at least thirty kilometres given the various sightings in different directions. Scientists now believe that many creatures have a 'bio-compass' that allows them to use the earth's magnetic field to navigate. Is that how she did it?

So many friends helped in the search for her that we decided to have a party. A group of us assembled in the dining room of a guesthouse in the village for Sunday lunch. Sarah, of course, was guest of honour. In between the entree and the main, a few people wandered out to the verandah to chat. And Sarah was with them—until, suddenly, she wasn't. She disappeared—again!

Everyone dispersed to start searching. So much for lunch. This time we weren't worried so much as furious. There was no sign of her that afternoon. Susan and I went home not quite believing what had happened.

The next day we were back in the village again, searching. We'd not been long there when a woman we knew called and said she had just spotted Sarah at a particular house. We were nearby so got there a minute or two later. We both saw her as soon as we entered the front yard. She approached gingerly, her usually pert fluffy tail tucked between her legs. She knew we were angry with her. She was filthy. I grabbed her and, instead of giving her a cuddle like last time, held her away from my body. Even Susan looked at her severely. We tossed her in the back of the car. She was in trouble!

She has never done it again.

*

This morning, before going over to Virginia Park, I went for a walk with Ginger and Bodhi. Sarah waited for Susan to get up.

It was a beautiful clear morning in our valley, with a fresh breeze from the west. Autumn has always been my favourite time in the Highlands.

The calves have been separated from their mothers for over a week and the mooing and complaining has stopped. The young ones are in the large paddock, enjoying the fresh green grass that has come up since all the rain. Freckle and one other cow are in the gully paddock below the house, and the other cows and Bill the bull are over the far side. All is as it should be in cattle heaven.

PART THREE

Chapter 22
Some Time Has Passed

Some time has passed since I wrote these stories about my animals, and read the many and varied writings of philosophers, scientists and others about our relationships with and perceptions of non-human animals. A great deal has changed in my life since then. But the solace and comedy that animals provide remain a constant.

The first big change was becoming a more serious farmer. And as it coincided with that period when our treatment of animals and our eating of them was much on my mind, it was not an altogether easy decision. The bargain I struck with myself was that I would give the cattle a good life. I would not sell the offspring until they had at least a couple of years of living contentedly with the herd, and I would not sell them into feedlots.

*

The charismatic but very odd cat Charlie—the one who followed me around like a dog and was a cooperative interlocutor in my attempts at animal communication—attacked me and put me in hospital. It wasn't really his fault. We knew—had been told when we adopted him—that he didn't get on with other cats. And one night, on the other side of the long lounge-room windows, he saw a feral cat in the garden. His reaction was extreme: hissing and yowling, his hackles raised.

I went close to see what was freaking him out and my footfall behind him pushed him over the edge. Suddenly all that aggression and hysteria was directed at me. He swung around and latched onto my leg. As I tried to shake him off blood was going everywhere. When I finally got him off me, he turned towards small Sarah. Susan snatched her up just in time.

While I was in hospital recovering, Susan found a new home for Charlie, somewhere where he would be an only pet and would never have to see another animal. My lifelong love of cats was put on hold.

Another shock to my confidence with animals came when I found my next horse, after Vincent went to live with Jenny.

Missy was the total opposite of Vincent. A huge seventeen-hands black mare with a placid temperament. She had lived in stables most of her life and was only taken out for dressage training or competitions. As she seemed happy with her limited life, I decided to keep her in the stables and gradually introduce her to a less sheltered way of living. In the meantime, I went to see her every other day to ride and groom her. Missy was what is called a 'school master', so well versed in dressage she 'taught' young beginning riders the discipline.

Just as we were getting used to each other and bonding more deeply, she came down with an acute bout of colic. Colic is the dread of any horse owner. I rushed her to the University of Sydney veterinary clinic at Camden, where they tried desperately to save her life. But after a night of drama and horror, Missy died.

The death of a horse affects me more powerfully even than that of my dog or cat. And I'm not sure why that is the case. I am often 'closer' with my dog, and a cat is usually far more demonstrative. But I usually bear their deaths better. Is it because with a horse you strike a kind of bargain? That they allow you to ride them, to join with them. And their death is not just the death of some 'other' but of a partner, a part of yourself. This might be fanciful but certainly Missy's death rocked me. I felt I failed her; I had not delivered that happier life.

*

Within the year, it was Susan's turn to end up in hospital, felled by a major stroke. This coincided with us building the new house at Virginia Park and me becoming a farmer. The bigger property didn't suit Susan as she struggled to regain her powers. She didn't have the strength to walk its beautiful paddocks. She couldn't do most of the things we had planned and anticipated.

A distance grew between us. Instead of bucolic bliss, we had some years of bitterness and rancour and little domestic harmony.

All this—our domestic situation, Charlie, Missy's death and the challenge of running a much bigger farm with ten times the number of cattle—meant I had little time or appetite for writing. As well, the scale of Victoria Park also meant losing some of my intimate contact with the farm animals, which had been a driving force for this book.

My only joy at this time came in the form, of course, of a new horse. Jake was given to me by the friend of a friend some months after Missy's death. He was an ex-racehorse, with a strong but forgiving temperament that seemed to match my own.

I approached him with no expectations. After Missy he was almost a joke, a small compact bay, and completely green in the ways of dressage. But he was handsome and had a certain arrogance that I appreciated. I did get help with his schooling because for several months after Susan's stroke I had little time to ride him myself. When I did start riding Jake regularly I resolved not to be guided by any coach. I'd done too much of that in the past. Whatever relationship developed between him and me, it had to be unmediated. Having no expectations allowed something lovely to flower between us. In the dressage arena, we were both very forgiving of each other's limitations. Outside it, he was happy to attempt to herd cattle. And nothing beat the joy of a gallop up the hill, where we'd stand and gaze at the view.

Virginia Park's gentle paddocks were easy country for cattle and humans. That had been one of its attractions. But out the back was the big hill and steep gullies, where kangaroos congregated and hidden streams trickled through the undergrowth. Riding through this area was like being somewhere far more remote. No sound but the wind in the trees.

*

Lina, of course, accompanied us to Virginia Park. On the day of the move, I took Jake and old Jim in the float together and had to go back to get Lina. She was waiting patiently at the barn. I led her to the trailer's ramp and she stopped and looked at it, clearly reluctant to go on. I didn't try to force her—a donkey is even less likely to respond to force than a horse. A big, burly bloke might have been able to shove her on but I didn't have one of those to hand. Instead, I spoke to her.

'Lina, there is no one here now. Everyone has gone over to VP.'

She watched me.

'The cows have gone over. Jim and Jake are there.'

Still she watched me.

'Either you get on the float or you stay here on your own.'

I pointed to the inside of the trailer and waited. She looked at it. Then walked up the ramp on her own. And stood quietly while I locked her in.

I always said she was the smartest animal I ever owned.

*

At Virginia Park the horses had large paddocks and stables, quite close to the house. One of the joys of the place was having the horses so close. At Keil-na-nain the barn had been a long trek up the hill, out of sight and sound of the house, and that had always made me a little uneasy.

At the new place, Lina had a small paddock of her own next to the garden. From our separate studies Susan and I could see her. When Susan came home from hospital after the stroke, one of the first things she wanted to do was groom Lina—she was as devoted to her as I was.

But Lina needed an equine companion. There was a horse sale at the local saleyards—not a place I would normally go to buy a horse. But I wasn't after a riding horse, just a pony, or miniature, that could be a friend for Lina. There was one little pony that caught my eye, a pretty black Shetland who peered out fearfully from beneath a thick bushy forelock. He stood in the furthest corner of his yard and watched everything going on about him with a kind of nervy intelligence. He clearly hadn't been handled; instead of tying his sale number to his mane they'd had to paint it on his rump with a spray can.

Of course I bought him. And somehow managed to get him home. He had a tuft of white hair on his spine, indicating a scar. I suspected he had probably been struck with a metal bar at some point in his short life. No wonder he was afraid of humans.

Lina was quite unimpressed by her new companion. It took time till she grudgingly accepted him. Dexter, as we named him, watched her constantly, as if learning the ways of the world from her. Often, when things were very bad in those difficult years, when I was delaying returning to the house, I'd sit with Lina in their stable and she would stand beside me and offer her consoling sympathy, while Dexter stood nearby, listening, as I talked to her.

One animal who definitely enjoyed the move to the big property was our bull, Bill. Instead of just a handful of cows, now he had a whole herd. I had help with handling the cattle. Peter had originally come to do fencing and stayed on to help run the farm. To make for ease of management we created a laneway that ran in a square around the property, with about a dozen paddocks on the outside of the square and three in the middle. This made it easy to move the cattle from one part of the property to another.

There was already a sweet small laneway that ran across the middle and was dotted with wattles and tea-tree. It was a favourite haunt of butterflies. We kept the cattle out of it and reserved it for walking and riding. We dubbed it Butterfly Lane. It was the only part of Virginia Park that Susan could walk with some ease and pleasure. In the course of the fencing, Peter, the new part-time manager of Virginia Park, positioned a log halfway along the lane so Susan could sit there a while. He did the same with the bigger laneways but they were mostly beyond her reach.

At the time, I was interested in the methods of American farming guru Joel Salatin. In more than a dozen popular books, which include *Folks, This Ain't Normal, You Can Farm* and *Salad Bar Beef*, he has described how he took a piece of neglected land and over several years increased its productivity exponentially, without ploughing or the use of artificial fertilisers. While the high-profile Salatin calls himself a 'lunatic farmer', *The New York Times* dubbed him the 'high priest of pasture' because of the importance he places on healthy grass. Salatin also emphasises sustainable farming and the interconnectedness of animals.

On his 220-hectare family farm in Swoope, Virginia, Salatin has used a very intensive form of rotational grazing, utilising not just cattle but also chickens. The paddocks were divided into tiny sections with electric fencing and the herd of cattle would be in each section only one day before being moved to the next, meaning the pasture was grazed heavily but over such a short space of time that the cattle didn't keep going over and over the same stretch of grass. The chickens came through afterwards, with their gypsy-caravan coop, and picked over the paddock. The chooks spread the cow manure as they scratched for grubs. In the process, they aerated the soil, created compost and aided the cycle of renewal, growth and creation of healthy pasture.

Peter was prepared to go along with many, if not all, of my enthusiasms. We were an odd partnership—me long and lanky, Peter short and stocky and twenty years my junior. But we worked well together. Neither Peter nor I was up to moving the cows every day, as Salatin recommended, or in putting up so much electric fencing, so we compromised on moving them once or twice a week, depending on the size of the paddock. The land responded. Not as fast as it might have if we'd spread the tonnes of superphosphate that the local agronomist advised, but I was interested in trying a different way.

Peter did build the 'mobile mineral bar' that I wanted. It was a small open-sided shed on sleds, containing several large tubs of minerals: the brilliant blue of copper sulphate, soft yellow sulphur, salt, dolomite. The 'sled' would be taken from paddock to paddock with the cows and they could free-feed on whichever minerals they felt in need of. Initially they really went for it, showing what they were in need of. Over time, they went to the mineral feeder less.

Spring was a busy time at the farm, with the cows dropping their calves sometimes two or three in a day, meaning the herd had to be checked regularly. Mostly everything went smoothly, but sometimes it didn't. Once a fox got to a calf so soon after calving that neither it nor its mother had time to get to their feet. The calf lost an eye and had some other injuries but survived. Peter and I weren't there that day. The calf was found by our friend J who lived in the cottage, who took him back to the barn to care for him. Uproar from Peter! 'The calf should have been left with its mother.' It would survive or not. Now we had a sickly, injured calf that would require months of attention. He survived but became difficult, not knowing whether he was related to humans or his herd.

A lot of cattle farmers arrange it so their cows calve in autumn, which means the calves can be weaned six months later in spring. They are then sold soon after to other farmers who have plenty of spring grass to fatten them, or kept for a few months to grow out a bit and sold before summer burns off the grass. Often they end up at the abattoir before their first birthday.

I couldn't in all conscience be a cattle farmer unless I gave them a longer life than that. And because our herd was small and the land good I was mostly able to do it. I didn't care for the idea of cows having to feed their calves through the hard winter months. In the Highlands it can be very hard and cold. So our cows calved in spring and the calves were weaned in early autumn. The cows were already back in calf by then, Bill having joined the herd around Christmas. All his Christmases literally did come at once.

Bill by this time was enormous, with a gorgeous rich chocolate coat and a lovely head topped by a cap of tight white curls. He was too big to fit in the cattle crush. (That makes it sound worse than it is—it's just a metal construction that an animal can be restrained in while they receive treatment.) But Bill was so quiet that you could walk up to him in the yard and give him an injection while he just stood there.

He was throwing some lovely calves. Once weaned, the steers had at least another year at the farm, usually longer. But the best of the heifers we kept; we were forming a second herd from Bill's offspring. That meant acquiring another bull.

Chapter 23
Complications

The stables at Virginia Park were directly behind the house, about forty metres away across the farm driveway. From the back door I could see Jake standing at his window and gazing expectantly towards me.

On one of our first mornings at Virginia Park I saddled up Jake just as the sun was rising and went out to inspect our new terrain from the saddle for the first time. Such was our bond that although everything was new to Jake, and potentially scary, we were on the same wavelength that spring morning; both seduced and calmed by the beauty of the day and the place where we found ourselves. Jake became my solace and escape. As the sun rose higher and there were distant sounds of the day getting underway, it was hard to turn towards home and the difficulties that always lay there.

My attitude towards the animals in these years was complicated. It would be easy to say that the three dogs were my constant companions: big golden Ginger and sweet, ever-faithful Bodhi, and little Sarah, Susan's fluff bucket of silky blonde hair. But in truth my mind was often elsewhere, and they were not farm dogs; they were not comfortable around a herd of cattle. Nor around the horses. So mostly they stayed in the house yard, except for their twice-daily walks. Susan often took them in the mornings on her slow progression to Butterfly Lane, and sometimes in the evening she and I managed an almost harmonious walk together, to the end of the long driveway and back, the dogs bounding along ahead or, in Sarah's case, walking sedately at Susan's heels.

In the mornings Bodhi and Ginger often accompanied me on a slow wander across the paddocks. We'd see small dark wallabies among the thickets of dense bush, or groups of big greys out on the open hillside, nibbling on dewy grass. We crossed the tracks of foxes that had passed this way in the night, leaving behind their pungent scent.

During the day Bodhi and Ginger were often in my study with me. They waited patiently for whatever attention I, with my distracted mind, might give them. There was no judgement in their gaze. The same could not be said for Sarah. She was Susan's shadow, devoted to her. Sometimes when I passed, Sarah would give me such a look of disappointment and disgust that I'd have to look away. It was clear whom she blamed for the atmosphere of acrimony and bitterness that had overtaken the house.

Sarah was the most unusual dog I've known, a very curious little character. Dogs are mostly so transparent in their emotions. Not so Sarah. Unlike with most dogs, I could never be sure what she was thinking. So it could be that attributing feelings of disgust and disappointment to her says more about my feelings of guilt than anything that was going on with her. She did sometimes look afraid of me, which always gave me pause. I was never angry with her but such was the symbiotic relationship she had with Susan that she took on board whatever vitriol was in the air. Dogs will do that.

But although they witnessed some terrible rows between Susan and me, they were also a rare part of our lives where we could meet with enjoyment. For brief spells they could restore harmony between us. And when they witnessed that harmony their joy was palpable. They played and gambolled like pups. It is almost heartbreaking to remember their innocence and what we put them through.

Those years at Virginia Park were such an uneven mixture of beauty, interest and misery that it is hard even now to settle on a final view of them. I loved the place with a passion, the animals large and small occupied me intensely and brought great satisfaction. But every small moment of joy or happiness had to be snatched and hoarded. Moments of peace occurred only when I was with Jake or alone in the landscape; early mornings on the verandah, wrapped in a blanket and with a cup of tea, watching the mist lift from the paddocks and the forms of cattle emerge; their lowing as they called their calves. And, behind me, the house silent—Susan still asleep.

*

By this time my attitude towards eating animals I had grown had shifted. All those years at Keil-na-nain I'd been happy enough to fatten steers and send them off to market, but squeamish about eating my own stock. That was changing. I was moving towards the view that it was preferable to eat one's own meat because you knew what sort of life the animal had had and what chemicals it had been exposed to. If I could have found a mobile butcher to do the butchering on the farm, I might have killed our own beef. But the other problem was that farm-butchered meat cannot leave the property and there was no way Susan and I could eat that much beef.

It was partly for this reason that we got some sheep. We chose Black Suffolk. With their pretty black heads and neat, compact bodies they were handsome and sweet-natured. They lived mostly in the driveway paddock where they kept the grass trimmed and were not tall enough to damage the trees. Within a year or so we needed to consider their future. I delayed. When they were approaching their second birthdays a decision had to be made. By this stage they were technically hoggets, known colloquially as 'two-teeth' because by then they have two adult teeth. While they are popular for the export market, hoggets are mostly considered too old for domestic consumption. We Australians like our lamb young and tender.

I arranged for the sheep to go to an abattoir less than an hour away. I wanted to make the journey as short and stress-free as possible.

Usually stock are taken in large trucks to the abattoir the day before, and kept in pens awaiting their fate. But Peter took ours in the horse float on the morning they were to die, and arranged for them to be first in the door. Maybe then the moment of trauma could be kept as brief as possible. Afterwards, a local butcher collected the carcasses and did the butchering. We kept the meat from two for ourselves. We ate it…but not all that enthusiastically.

Chapter 24
A Very Hard Decision

Five years after we bought Virginia Park, after the worst times were behind us and Susan and I were reconciled, I made one of the hardest decisions I've ever made. I decided to sell the place I loved so much. I knew Susan could never be happy there—it represented the period of her greatest misery. She never liked the house we'd built. The size and space of both the house and the farm mocked her; every hour exposed the limitations of her body.

But she never pressured me about selling—my attachment was so obvious. We had planned to stay for ten to fifteen years. If a decision was ever made to leave earlier, it would have to be mine.

Over time, as we re-found the bonds between us, the size and isolation of VP began to mock me. What was the point of such a place if it wasn't shared? It was absurd that I should rattle around there on my own.

It crystallised one late afternoon when I was riding Jake back towards our little settlement of barns, cottages and homestead. It was autumn and the leaves of the deciduous trees were turning various shades of yellow, gold and deepest claret. As the sun dropped, the tall pines threw long shadows across red roofs. The horse shelters and neat paddocks, the trimmed hedges, the very track I rode on. All of it I was responsible for; the saving of the old and the building of the new. It had never looked more beautiful. Could I leave it? And suddenly I knew I must.

It was another two years before we finally moved. I had plenty of time to say my farewells, and the life of the farm continued unchanged: calves were born and were weaned; steers sold. Our new, young bull, Gavin, sired his first offspring. And when he and Bill were not with their respective herds they shared a paddock quite companionably.

By the time we left Virginia Park we were reduced to two dogs—Sarah and Bodhi. We had lost our big golden girl, Ginger, another casualty of hip dysplasia. Another dog passing, another grave in the garden. If only we could all be buried in our gardens.

The hardest part of leaving, the only really tough day, was the day the cows left. Peter had arranged for them to be sold to another property in the area, so they didn't have to go through the saleyards; so they would stay together. I was with them at the yards, but when the truck backed up to the loading ramp and they started to clatter aboard, I had to turn away.

The only equines we could take with us when we moved to two acres in the village were Lina and Dexter. Jake would have to be boarded at an equestrian centre nearby, and I wasn't sure how he'd take to it. But he settled in fine and seemed to find great interest in being surrounded by so many horses and so much activity.

So Susan and I, Sarah and Bodhi, and Lina and Dexter settled into our new life 'in town'. The first thing that struck me was that I now had leisure. It was astounding. I couldn't remember ever having real leisure before, because when you have a lot of animals there is always something that needs to be done, someone who needs attending to. We now had a small lap swimming pool and I remember floating on my back and thinking 'so this is what it's like!'

Sarah, meanwhile, was ageing. The house in the village has a tiled gallery, where the dogs slept, and it was a good thing it was tiled because in the mornings I started finding little 'gifts' that Sarah had deposited overnight. Cleaning up Sarah's shit first thing in the morning was not a good start to the day but there wasn't much alternative—Susan slept on for a good hour after the rest of us were awake.

But it was clear Sarah was going downhill and this was particularly hard on Susan, such was the bond between them. When Susan had the stroke, she didn't realise what was happening; it took Sarah's reaction to make her realise. Sarah looked at her intently, as if to say *Get up! Get help NOW*. So insistent was her gaze that Susan forced herself off the bed and somehow got herself to the back door and called for me before she collapsed and lost her speech. Ever since, it had been evident that Sarah felt a responsibility to look after Susan. When they went for their slow walks around the lanes Sarah was always at her heels. It looked like the dog was taking the human for a walk, not the other way around.

We were trying to make a decision about Sarah; she was getting increasingly incontinent and weaker. We waited for a sign from her, signalling that she had had enough. It was a hard time.

Out of the blue, Susan suggested we should get a kitten. I was surprised as she is not really a cat person. We hadn't had a cat since I was attacked by Charlie years ago at Keil-na-nain. I think we both felt we were surrounded by ageing critters: Sarah and Bodhi were both seventeen, Lina was starting to suffer from ill health, Jake had bad knees after his former life as racehorse. We needed new life around. And a kitten would be the 'bundle of joy' that might distract and console us upon Sarah's demise.

One day Susan passed me the local paper and pointed at an ad from the cat shelter. The photo showed a cute half-grown white and tortoiseshell kitten. Whoever wrote their ads knew exactly how to tug at the heartstrings. The one for 'Barney' read: 'I'm the last of my litter. Everyone else has gone to their forever-homes. I'm waiting for my family to come for me. Maybe no one is ever going to come.'

'I'm coming Barney, I'm coming!' Susan gasped, wailed, and rushed for the phone.

So we ended up with Barney. And it was exactly as predicted. He was a constant delight and distraction. He'd lived at the cat shelter until he was five months old and as a result was a very sociable cat. He was also accustomed to the shelter volunteers putting him in his cage and going home at 5pm, not returning until 8am the next day. So he was no trouble at night. He would go into 'his' room (for a while the back bedroom) even before the television was turned off, and wouldn't make a peep until he was let out the next morning.

Chapter 25
A Last Move

After leaving Virginia Park I missed the space, the landscape—those long vistas across the paddocks—and the silence. But most of all I missed the cows. Their gentle presence and occasional playfulness, their soothing contentment as they lay about under the big oak tree in front of the house, chewing cud. I couldn't drive past a paddock of Herefords without slowing and peering at them. Looking for distinctive markings, wondering if any of them might be related to my girls.

I was lucky we hadn't moved to the city. I was still surrounded by trees and open space. We had a small old orchard and vegie beds. There were cows not far away, horses just down the road, and Lina and Dexter in the paddock behind the house. And once we had a pen for them, we got some chooks.

Jenny and her husband Ian (and Vincent) were a five-minute drive away. And Jan was back living with us again, in the original cottage on our block. We'd had a break from each other for a few years while Susan and I were at Virginia Park. But she had been missing Lina—she was not so sure about us! Before long, Jan's mare Chelsea also rejoined us.

Jake was facing retirement as his arthritic knees were deteriorating and Chelsea would be company for him. Later we managed to acquire the paddock next door, an extra two acres for their retirement paddock. That meant Jake could come home on and off from the equestrian centre. Susan dubbed our new place 'Little Farm'.

*

I started to look for a new horse to ride. I was quite sure, this time, what type of horse I was looking for. After Vincent, Missy and Jake, all very different, at last I knew what would suit me and why.

When I saw Leo's ad in a horse magazine I knew immediately he was what I was after. He was six years old—a good age. He was a tad under sixteen hands, the same as Jake. He even looked like Jake. But his breed was interesting, a Cleveland Bay, an old English breed used for both riding and carriage work. They are known as the English warm blood and are quite rare in Australia. I even liked his name.

He was at a trainer's about three hours away. The first impression was good. He was a rich red bay with a beautiful black tail. He had a very alert expression, always taking in everything around him. For a young horse he had done quite a bit: novice dressage, lots of training clinics with his owner. I didn't meet his owner—her marriage had broken up and she was being forced to sell him.

The day I went to see Leo I didn't take anyone with me for a second opinion, I rode him only once, I didn't get a vet check (which one normally does to make sure they are sound). I liked him and he wasn't expensive. I wasn't going to find another as good any time soon. So Leo came to live at the equestrian centre, Shibumi, a ten-minute drive from where I'd been keeping Jake.

*

In our early years in the Highlands, summers were often cool and misty. The first year I don't think I wore a T-shirt all summer and Christmas was so cool we had to light the wood burner. It was commonly said in the Highlands that one never slept without a blanket. But things had changed. There were a couple of very hot summers at Virginia Park, with day after day in the high thirties. Then came the Black Summer of 2019/20.

Our small paddocks were bare and brown. The air was full of smoke. The paddocks at the equestrian centre were similarly denuded. The fire front was a good thirty kilometres away; there was no immediate danger. But to both the north and the south of us there were out-of-control fires and during the afternoon a huge pyrocumulus cloud had developed. Just before dark I went outside and I didn't have a good feeling.

The horses were alert but not nervous. They were in their familiar surroundings. But they were confined and that confinement could be fatal if there were a fire. The best thing for paddock animals when there's a fire is to give them as much space and options for escape as possible. I decided to put them all out. Jake, Chelsea and Leo were safer at Little Farm, I thought, and were put out in the new two-acre paddock. There was barely a blade of grass, so if a fire did come through there wouldn't be much to burn. The three horses were not accustomed to being in a paddock together. But they stood calmly watching me as I closed the gate, as if nonplussed.

I put Lina and Dexter in the two small paddocks behind the house and opened the gates so they could move between them—with luck they'd be able to move away from any flames. I opened the door of the chicken coop. Then I went inside and told Susan I thought maybe we should take the cat and dog and go. As I did so, the landline was ringing, and an emergency message came up on my phone. We were being told to evacuate.

Jan appeared as I was putting Barney into his cage. We already had bags packed and near the car.

'You're coming, too,' I said to Jan.

'No, I'll stay and help the firies,' she said. She would not be dissuaded. While I, usually calm, had gone into a panic, Jan, quite often anxious, had assumed a steely calm.

We headed off into a night made even darker by the thick smoke. By this time the only vehicles on the road were fire trucks.

When we arrived at the Moss Vale Services Club there was a stream of people going in, most of them with dogs and quite a few with cats. The club became crowded but the animals were all very well behaved. Bodhi sat beside me on the carpet in the lounge, panting a little. Barney crouched in his cage. The club staff went around with glasses of water for the humans and bowls of water for the animals.

The first thing I had to do the next morning was go to the nearest supermarket and get Barney a litter tray—I'd neglected to pack that! He was hanging on.

*

In recent months Lina had started going downhill. She lost weight and started being picky with her food. Tests were done; I've lost track of the number of tests. A string of medications. Nothing seemed to help; she kept losing weight. The terrible heat of that summer didn't help either. Sometimes I put a wet sheet over her to cool her as she stood morosely in the paddock. I'd sit with her and talk to her. It was very bad.

One day I said to her: 'If it's too hard, Lina, you don't have to keep going.' But I got the very strong message that she wasn't ready to give up.

Over a few weeks she gradually picked up. She ate more, she looked brighter. Then had come the fires. After our first evacuation the smoke, heat and tension remained. We were all constantly on alert and the animals must have felt it.

One morning Jan came to the kitchen door just as I was making my first cup of tea for the day. She has always been a very early riser.

'I think you had better come and have a look at Lina.'

We went out to the small paddock behind the barn, where Lina was mooching around looking for non-existent grass. Straight away I saw the problem: from under her tail—coming from her anus or vagina, I couldn't tell which—protruded a pinkish sack of flesh about twenty centimetres in length. She came towards me, looking quite bright. I had some carrot tops in my hand—they'd become one of the few things that would tempt her. She took her carrot tops, apparently oblivious to the terrible business coming out of her behind.

I called John. He was with us within the hour. His wife Wendy and the twins were with him.

'Prolapsed rectum,' he said. I looked at him, expecting him to say how he would fix it. 'It's not worth trying, Annie.'

I looked at Lina standing in the stable, seeming a bit resigned at having yet another visit from the vet, but otherwise a lot better than she had often been in recent weeks.

'Couldn't you operate?'

'I could. But I don't think it would do much good and I don't think she's up to it.'

I was shocked.

'You need to make a decision because with that mass hanging out of her...' He didn't have to say any more—I'd seen a flyblown horse in the past.

'Would you come back later in the day?'

'I could...but sooner would be better.'

'I have to tell Susan.'

I went back to the house through a veil of tears. I couldn't grasp it—it was too sudden.

Lina had been quite calm while Jan and I, and John and Wendy, were with her. But as soon as she saw Susan her expression changed. It was as if she knew at that moment. She tried to pull the lead from Jan's hand, to leave the stable, to get away from us. Susan put a hand on Lina's forehead and wept. Then we led her out to the far corner of the paddock. All this was watched by the other horses. Jake was nearest. He stood in his yard staring at us.

She resisted, she resisted the whole way. Jan and I led her, Susan and Wendy trailed behind. John prepared the syringe. The little boys were playing under the walnut tree on the other side of the barn, as if protecting themselves from what was happening in the paddock.

When we got to the spot, Jan and I had to really hang onto Lina. There was no time to talk to her, beyond a few endearments. No time to explain. I should have tried harder. She didn't understand about the prolapse, but she would have before the day was out, when the flies began to swarm, when maggots formed. It was like I could hear a voice coming from her: *But I feel okay! Don't do this—I don't want to go!*

So strong and stubborn did she become at the end that Jan and I were struggling to hold her still so John could get the needle in. I felt like I fought her till her last breath. In the background, Susan and Wendy were crying. Wendy! I'd always thought her such a tough nut, but she turned away, saying 'This is what I can't handle.'

Jan and I hung on until our Lina sank to the ground. In the yards, Jake stood still as a statue, watching.

We were all traumatised by the loss of Lina, humans and equines. There were many times when I had sought her company when the pressure of human relationships weighed too heavily; when I would sit in the paddock or stable with her and she would approach and stand by me. Ruffling my hair with her muzzle or resting her head on my shoulder. Nothing needed to be said.

We tried hard to save her. In the end nothing could be done.

Chapter 26
In Times of Crisis

Amid all the drama, poor little Dexter the Shetland was almost forgotten. He had lost his mate when Lina died and he felt it keenly. It was some months before we realised just how miserable he was, when the grief started to affect him physically.

It was a beautiful spring with plenty of rain. So different from the year before. The only worry was Dexter, lonely and morose after Lina's death. We found him a companion, another elderly Shetland called Rosie. She was company but she wasn't a friend—not the way that Lina had been. She was bossy.

Dexter wasn't doing well. He had developed laminitis, even though Jan, in particular, was so strict with his feed. His feet were looking more and more misshapen. The farrier didn't seem to know what to do with them. I was convinced the problem was more than his feet and what we were feeding him. I called in Angela the herbalist and she did a hair test. Will it surprise anyone if I say she diagnosed grief? It didn't surprise me. He also had a very sluggish metabolism, for which she prescribed magnesium. We started feeding him more, not less, to get his system moving. And ginger tea, and homeopathy. And perhaps most importantly I found a farrier who had a knack with laminitic ponies.

Within weeks Dexter and his feet were on the mend. More than that, he was happier. Out in the paddock he'd break into a canter and kick up his heels. People often think that laminitis in horses is just caused by what the animal is eating. But stress can also be a cause, and Dexter had had a very stressful year. We all had, and it wasn't over yet.

*

I'd been having a bit of trouble with my left arm, occasional pain up near the shoulder. And weeks before I'd made an appointment with a very good physiotherapist—I had to wait five weeks to get in to see him.

He manipulated it, trying to work out what might be the problem. That really made my arm ache. Then he said I should get an ultrasound of the lump.

So I did.

Then I was told I should have a biopsy.

So I did.

He told me I had a sarcoma, a rare form of cancer.

It didn't sound all that serious. But a day or two later, while leading Leo back to his paddock after riding him, I was hollowed out by an ominous premonition.

After seeing the specialist, I went straight into a series of scans and appointments. After each one the news got worse. By the end of the week our lives had been turned upside down.

I was to have five weeks of radiotherapy and an operation six weeks later to replace the shoulder joint. Although the surgeon was upbeat, it was pretty clear my arm and shoulder would never be the same.

I rode Leo for another couple of weeks, until near the time when radiotherapy was to start. By then the arm was really bothering me. I brought him home from the equestrian centre. I wanted him close, I wanted to be able to see him and the others whenever I was home.

The radiotherapy started just after new year. During it I began to think about the long months of rehabilitation that would come after the operation. Susan was being wonderful, but I would need another companion on the journey. I would need a dog.

Every dog is different and we relate to each dog in somewhat different ways; also, in our lifetime there may be one dog who stands out from all the rest. Yet, despite this, it is also true that there is something unchanging about having a dog in your life. That sense of connection and contentment gets repeated time after time with each dog. It is the reason why the only real solution to being heartbroken by the death of a dog is to get another dog.

When I told Susan I wanted to get a puppy, she said the timing was all wrong. I said the timing was just right. I had worked it out. I would have six weeks between the end of radiotherapy and the operation. Six weeks to teach the pup some manners and the rules of the house. After that, the pup would need to be able to contain his or her exuberance and be a gentle and respectful companion to me while I recuperated. Susan could not dissuade me.

I found a pup of indeterminate breeding that had been rescued by the RSPCA. At first glance she was black and white, but on closer inspection her coat was somewhere between black and chocolate brown, and very fine. She was smooth as a seal. I called her Suki. She was thirteen weeks old. Good friends made an eight-hour round-trip journey to the Hunter Valley to collect her for me.

It didn't take long to work out that what Suki wanted most in life was to be good, and to be praised for it. And that she was very smart and learnt her lessons quickly. Within a couple of days she knew some basic rules—where in the house she was allowed and where she was not. And what furniture she was allowed to sit on, like the armchair in my study. And what she was not allowed on, like the cream sofa in the sitting room. The thing she most liked to sit on was a lap. That hasn't changed, even though she now weighs twenty-five kilos.

The first word I taught her was 'gentle' because that was what she was going to have to be.

*

A scan showed the radiotherapy hadn't worked—the tumour hadn't shrunk. It was too risky to try to do the operation they'd planned.

In the end there was no alternative: the arm would have to be amputated. I took this news with the kind of stunned calm that sometimes manifests in extreme situations. I had ten days to get used to the idea. I spent a lot of it with the animals. And the rest of the time on Susan's computer editing her latest manuscript. I wanted to get it done before the operation. 'While I still have two hands,' I said. We both laughed at the crazy tragi-comedy of it all.

As always, I showed my true feelings only with the animals. On one dark day I lay on the bed with Barney, sobbing and wailing. Rather than fleeing this banshee, Barney snuggled in and purred louder and louder as if trying to drown out my sobs with his reassuring warmth.

A few days before the operation I sat in the barn with the horses. By this time, Leo and Jake were such good mates that they often stood in the stable together. I was in what had been Lina's stable but was now Dexter's. I put a milk crate down and sat on it, my back against the half wall that divided the stables. There wasn't much to say and, as always with the animals, words were not the point. But I told the boys I was sorry, that I wasn't sure how much I'd be able to do with them after this was over. Jake and Leo reached over the partition and snuffled my hair, one at each ear. Dexter stood facing me and stared at me, his liquid brown eyes steady under his bushy forelock.

We stayed like that for some time.

*

The first three weeks after the amputation were bad. When I came home from hospital, I was weak, I was thin. Our friend CJ arrived from New Zealand to see me on one of the first flights allowed during a brief trans-Tasman travel bubble during Covid. I leant on his chest and wept, remembering our many rides together over those grand bald hills of the Wairarapa. I wasn't sure if I would ever do it again.

But I still had my right arm. And I was, luckily, naturally dexterous. I just had to learn a few new skills. And I was spared the months of rehabilitation that would have followed a shoulder replacement. I had to just get on with it.

I set myself a goal: to be back on Leo six weeks from the date of the operation. My coach Sally-Ann had been coming to ride him for the past month. She was getting him accustomed to being ridden one-handed. Leo was unperturbed.

Suki, meanwhile, was a constant delight. She still sometimes leapt up on other people but she never did it to me. Even when very excited, when she rushed at me exuberantly, she would skid to a stop at my feet and sit very straight and wait for that ultimate compliment: 'Good girl.'

When I was sitting down, she invariably wanted to be in my lap. In those early days I'd sit in the window seat in the dining room to watch the sunrise and she would be by my feet at the other end of the seat. Very still and expectant as I drank my tea and ate my toast. Just after sunrise I'd usually see Jan making her way to the barn to let the horses out. It was comforting to be surrounded by these normal routines. As

I finished my toast, Suki would creep onto my lap to receive the last crust. Then stay there, snuffling and licking me.

Within a week or two I worked out how to put head-collars on the horses, although I'd had to get new head-collars that could be managed with one hand. Jake was cooperative, giving his head a little shake at just the right moment so the head-collar settled into place. Leo was more playful, but also bore with me as I utilised all I had—hand, knee, teeth. By the second or third time he understood what was required.

Putting on the horses' rugs was trickier, in particular the multiple clasps and buckles. Jake had never been a patient horse but now he seemed to understand. He just stood in his yard, immovable, as I fiddled and fiddled and tried to work out how to do this. The bridle was easier. But putting the saddle on was beyond me. Luckily, willing helpers were around to help me saddle up. As planned, I rode Leo six weeks from the day of the op. We even cantered. I was grinning like a twelve year old.

*

I have tried to answer the question I posed at the beginning of this book. 'What do animals mean to us?' in multiple ways, citing research, my own experience, my own thoughts, and introducing you to various animals I have loved and observed closely. Also to the lives of other animals including Alex the parrot, Brenin the wolf, Christian the lion and that extraordinary dog Strongheart.

But answers are unknowable, despite advances in our knowledge. The ties and connections we have with other species remain wonderfully mysterious, beyond analysis in words or scientific experiment. What is certain is that animals weave themselves not just into our hearts but into the fabric of our lives. Their sheer physicality is reassuring; they are so *in* their skins. And maybe that is why I relate to them. A former partner used to call me 'Cat', and I don't think it was just because of my affinity with them. They are languid, intimately connected to the physical world but also self-contained.

The smell of a horse's skin, the roughness of a calf's tongue, the happy horror of a dog's lick. These are stored in my memory, as much a part of me as any other sensation the world has to offer. Now, with Suki, I am reminded daily of the joy of their simple connection with the world. When my legs entwine with hers as we fight for space on the sofa, we are engaged in a dance between species. Exploring and enjoying.

Animals are both more complicated than they are given credit for but also, often, wonderfully simple. Just as with people, not every relationship is perfect; sometimes they can turn sour. But if so, it is often because we have brought to the relationship some expectation that they cannot or simply don't want to meet.

When we take on the responsibility of an animal—be it a rabbit or a cow or a cat—it is another creature we must care for outside ourselves. We can never really know their experience of the world, even when we share a space with them. Ultimately they are in our power, this living creature that we watch and wonder about but can never really know.

If you approach without judgement, they will return the favour. I realise it is a lesson I learnt as a child and one I've tried to carry into my human relationships. To worry about a problem with an animal just makes it worse. And I think the same is true of people.

In my new, altered life, being with my animals is both restful and engaging. They tie one to the present. That is more important now than ever.

Afterword
by Susan Varga, Anne's partner of thirty-three years

One year after her diagnosis with a rare sarcoma in her arm, Anne died at home, in December 2021.

In the last year of her life, she tried to finish *Our Familiars*. She also made notes for additional material when she could no longer write.

Knowing that she was so close to finishing, she asked me and Joyce Morgan, one of her oldest and best friends, to tie up loose ends and make small changes after her death. Joyce and I are also writers, so she was confident we could manage the task.

Joyce has done some extra research along the lines Anne wanted. I have made some edits and a few necessary additions. Otherwise the book is wholly Anne's.

It has been my pleasure and joy—together with Joyce—to bring Anne's last book into the reading world.

The joy has been admixed with much pain. Anne's death shocked everyone who knew her. She was an active, healthy woman of sixty-four. In 2019 we got married, not long after the successful referendum on same-sex marriage. We recommitted to a future together.

In this afterword—rarely has a word been used so literally—I want to tell you, from my point of view, how Anne's relationship with animals was magnified and deepened in her last year of life.

Anne always had a strong premonition that she was going to die young. From her youth she had held onto a romantic notion that she would die at the age of forty-two. That date came and went, but she never wanted to grow old and endure losing her mental and physical powers.

So when the first diagnosis came, she was already warning me that she might die. She was not shocked by the thought. When radiation failed to shrink the lump in her arm, she started to prepare. Her practical brain told her we needed a new puppy to divert us and get us through the months ahead.

We were going through a time without dogs. Our beloved trio of adopted older dogs had died: Ginger first, then our eccentric, unreadable Sarah at eighteen. Then quiet, sensible Bodhi, a true gentleman, aged nineteen.

All dog lovers dread a dog's death, because dogs' lives are much shorter than ours. Anne did not want to record every death that spanned the years in this book, yet I want to tell about Sarah's death. This small 'fluff bucket', as Anne called her, had been a big character and her death was as singular as she was.

We were up in our winter retreat, our weatherboard cottage in Brunswick Heads on the north coast of New South Wales, with our two dogs, and the two horses boarded nearby with Northern Sally.

Sarah was becoming more and more incontinent with some kind of gut problem, but she hung on, indomitable. So we kept on cleaning up her wees and poos. It wasn't constant—she did try hard, but her system was shutting down. We waited, as we always did, for a sign that the dog's will was fading. But Sarah was obstinate. Repeatedly her body language said, *No! Not yet.*

Then, on the morning after a particularly bad night—the kitchen was awash—I picked her up and her frail little body told me very clearly, *I've had enough, Mum. It's time.*

We made an appointment for the vet that afternoon. For weeks Sarah had been fractious and anxious, but after that morning she became serene, calm and submitted to (and enjoyed) a gentle brush of her fine golden fur. When the time came to drive her to the vet, I wrapped her in a towel and she nestled in my lap peacefully.

At the vet's she had always hated the cold steel table, but that afternoon it did not matter. She lay quietly, cradled in our arms. She seemed to breathe a small sigh of relief as the needle went in. We waited.

The vet said, 'She's gone.'

I let out a howl of anguish, as if she was torn from my body.

Yet minutes later, as we left the surgery without her, on the path to the gate I felt her soul fly into my heart. She nestled in there, where she still lives. In my internal language, Sarah lies curled up, asleep.

Anne has taken up residence in the rest of my heart. She is still bursting with life, ready for action, even if death, like her missing arm, is a small hindrance to further adventures.

*

When Anne first brought up the subject of a new puppy at our time of crisis, I was appalled. How could we manage with my one arm affected by stroke and the other with arthritis; her with a useless arm, with the real possibility of losing it altogether? How would we feed, train and walk a puppy?

She said, breezily, 'I will find a puppy right now and I will train her to not jump up on me, and she will be a great diversion.'

So Suki came into our lives: a rescue dog, black and white, with a glossy coat, all energy and love. She has been an excellent 'diversion' – intelligent, demanding but offering loads of affection.

She and Anne developed a daily routine of togetherness. Suki was affectionate to everyone as most puppies are, but Anne was her beacon, leader, educator, playmate, her sun and stars. They spent a lot of time together, as if they both knew their time was short. Rowdy with others, Suki was always 'gentle' with Anne; her early training was embedded. The only time she forgot herself a little was when they fought for space on the daybed, entangling their long limbs together.

Barney, our rescue cat, a handsome and good-natured creature, also played a big role in making Anne's life rich, just as she was losing it. I'm convinced that any observant animal knows when their owners are in pain, physical or mental, and responds in their own ways. Barney was constantly around with extra purrs, knowing when he was needed.

*

All her life Anne had unconsciously or consciously employed animals to share her darkest emotions with them. She was quite frank in admitting that it mostly was her 'familiars' who saw her tears or despair. She could face the human world with composure because she had already had a commune with her animals to give her courage.

'Susan was wonderful but I needed something more,' as she wrote in the last few months.

I was not offended by this dismissive sentence on my efforts to nurse and comfort her. I knew Anne. Well before this crisis, I sometimes referred to myself, only half jokingly, as the Chief Pet and told her that I was working hard to retain my top ranking. Sometimes I wondered if the current horse or new dog had, secretly, top billing.

A scene comes back to me from the time when I was slowly recovering from my stroke. Not long afterwards, I broke my wrist in a fall and needed to be showered for a couple of weeks, and the task fell to Anne. She was clearly uncomfortable and irritated by this job, and I was feeling degraded and exposed.

Then I had a flash of inspiration. 'Imagine I'm a horse,' I said to her. 'You are hosing down your horse.'

She paused, and her face changed and relaxed. The human complications of our situation fled. Showering became a simple act of help and comfort between two creatures – her preferred state of being. A lesson I learnt then which has stood me in good stead.

There is a truly serious side to this anecdote. In Anne's world the crux of human and animal interactions was this: humans care for, feed and keep their animals safe; in return the animals give true companionship, cooperation and a sense of safety and mutual trust. I, as her partner, might be 'wonderful' but Anne also needed something else, at a level beyond speech.

In this she was always on the right track. She didn't need the research to show her what she understood from direct experience. As a result, she was not surprised by the recent research which has piled up in the last few years. We know now that animals are true caregivers and are being recognised as such more and more. In nursing homes, they comfort the residents. The lives of war veterans are turned around once they acquire well-trained dogs as companions. Many lonely and isolated people bloom once they care for an animal and vice versa. In prison programs, prisoners who train young dogs for the vision impaired change remarkably in their ability to adapt to prison life and after release.

Nowhere was it more striking than in Anne's last year, with her horses. Of course, she was scared and anxious about her arm being amputated, but she planned ahead, determined that she was not going to stop riding. Some years ago she stopped competing in dressage, and started riding simply for pleasure. The subtle interactions between horse and rider became a true passion. It was her meditation.

My persistent memory of her is her innocent half-smile when she was executing a dressage exercise with Leo. Totally absorbed, in a private world.

Anne had two horsey women in her life, both called Sally—Northern Sally, who lives in Northern Rivers, and Southern Sally, who lives in the Highlands. While Anne was in hospital for the amputation, Southern Sally started to train Leo to respond to one rein only, so Anne could get back on a horse again. Six weeks later, to the day, Anne rode Leo around the front paddock. Jan, Anne's sister Jenny, Southern Sally and I were all there with our hearts in our mouths.

Leo was impeccable and calm. They were a team. A small video of the event spread like wildfire among excited friends throughout the world. Despite losing half her shoulder as well as her left arm, Anne's natural balance helped her to control that large beast called a horse. The local horse community was behind her, too, helping her get on and off and keeping an eye out for falls.

The day Anne first rode Leo she felt herself again—she had achieved her goal. Learning to type and drive with one arm soon followed. Her ability to adapt was remarkable.

Good friends were giving support and practical help. But the essential team was her dog, the cat, Dexter the Shetland and the Chief Pet.

*

Eleven months after the initial prognosis, Annie's heart specialist told us Anne only had two to four weeks left to live. She was allowed to go home to die.

Two scenes from this time stand out: at home, Anne began to organise. One day out of the blue she said to me, 'I want you to go out and get a sofa; a two-and-a-half-seat sofa'.

I looked at her in amazement. 'Why? We don't need one. We have the two chairs in the TV room. No way. I am spending all my time with you, not chasing a bloody sofa.'

'It's important,' she said. 'You will need a sofa when I die so you and Suki can cuddle together in the evenings.'

So I found a sofa in the nearest town. We tested it out with the growing pup between us and held hands across Suki's young body.

'Okay,' I said, 'it was a good idea.'

Later, that sofa, with Suki beside me, was a lifeline for bearing Anne's loss.

The other thing that stands out in my memory was something I realised only later. Every evening after dinner, even as she got weaker, Anne went out to the horses to give them half a biscuit of hay and commune a little with them. She kept her old Ugg slippers on the verandah for the short trip to the stables.

In the last two months she went out earlier and earlier as she became more and more exhausted. One night she stopped going. She did not go the next night. She left the Ugg slippers in disarray at the door.

That's when I knew that she was dying.

*

As I and her friends were planning Anne's Celebration—no one wanted to use the word funeral for someone who had been so alive, vital and had just turned sixty-five—my friend Bronwyn said, 'A horse must feature in it.' Of course!

We talked to Sheryl at Shibumi, who said 'no problem'. She would provide the horse and carriage, and she would drive it. The local hall where we lived was the venue and it faces an oval. After the funeral, mourners gathered on the verandah.

A small carriage appeared with a white pony driven by Sheryl. On the back was Southern Sally carrying the urn. The pony and carriage did a lap of honour on the oval. The horse was a little frisky character, which made people laugh; Anne, too, was known for a streak of rebellion.

But everyone fell silent as the lap of honour ended and the horse slowed. Even the non-horsey people had tears in their eyes as the white horse, and the carriage bearing Anne's ashes, disappeared among the trees.

Very gradually, I am sorting out Annie's things. But I will never remove the old Ugg slippers lying on the verandah. They talk to me about the love and respect she gave her horses and dogs, and the love and respect they gave her back.

An Update
The Cast of Animals (and Two Humans)

Jake

Jake was pining without Anne, and he thought it would be beneath him to bond with the ponies. So Northern Sally came to the rescue, wanting to do something for Anne, her great friend. She suggested life in a warmer climate would suit Jake's arthritic legs. He has settled happily there and is enjoying the occasional ride.

Dexter

Dexter has bonded with Rosie. With Jake gone north, these days they have a stable each. Despite age and various ills, Dexie hangs on, and is getting a little less shy, more secure with his place in the family.

Jan (human)

Jan is back next door, after some years away, at Little Farm, tending the Shetlands and looking after Barney whenever needed. She misses Lina, as I do.

Leo

Anne's last horse, Leo, is at Shibumi. Anne asked Southern Sally to sell Leo. His new owner has kept him at Shibumi.

Vincent and Chelsea

Vincent is the true survivor of all our animals. He is living out his old age with Jenny, with whom he has a mutual love affair. He enjoys bossing his companion, Chelsea, Jan's pretty mare, who is also living to a sturdy old age.

Barney and Suki

Barney and Suki both spend daily time in Anne's study, on her office chair and her armchair.

After Anne's death, Suki conducted a campaign. She was determined to sleep at night on the daybed where she and Anne used to have their daily naps. I wouldn't let her. She remained unsettled and unhappy until I finally gave in.

The Chief Pet

I have Suki for company, and we cuddle every night on the new sofa in front of the TV, as instructed.

Notes

1 Charles Darwin, *The Expression of the Emotions in Man and Animals*, John Murray, London, 1872, p. 357.
2 ibid., p. 362.
3 ibid., p. 366.
4 S. Hughes and C. Gardner-Thorpe, 'Charles Bell's (1774–1842) contribution to our understanding of facial expression', *Journal of Medical Biography*, vol. 30, no. 4, 2022, pp. 206–214. doi:10.1177/0967772020980233
5 Anonymous, *Domesticated Animals; Considered with reference to Civilization and the Arts*, John W. Parker, London, 1837, p. 3.
6 ibid., p. 6.
7 ibid., p. 10.
8 C. Barras, 'Oldest dog burial suggests prehistoric humans loved dogs as pets', *New Scientist*, 8 February 2018, www.newscientist.com/article/2160695-oldest-dog-burial-suggests-prehistoric-humans-loved-dogs-as-pets/ and https://www.livescience.com/earliest-evidence-dog-domestication-arabian-peninsula.html.
9 J. Allen Boone, *Kinship with All Life*, Harper & Row, New York, 1954, p. 34.
10 ibid., p. 55.
11 ibid., p. 59.
12 ibid., p .68.
13 K. Mieszkowski, 'Don't have a cow!', *Salon*, 18 April 2009, www.salon.com/2009/04/18/masson_interview/.
14 'Andrew McLean—working with elephants', *The Horse Magazine*, 11 October 2012, www.horsemagazine.com/thm/2012/10/andrew-mclean-working-with-elephants/.
15 See E.P. Evans, *The Criminal Prosecution and the Capital Punishment of Animals*, William Heinemann, London, 1906.

16 Anon., *Domesticated Animals*, p. 48.
17 M. Hambly, 'Why do cats purr?', *New Scientist*, no date, www.newscientist.com/question/why-do-cats-purr/#:~:text=While%20purring%20is%20thought%20to,event.
18 N. Fleming, 'Hungry cats trick owners with baby cry mimicry', *New Scientist*, 13 July 2009, https://www.newscientist.com/article/dn17455-hungry-cats-trick-owners-with-baby-cry-mimicry/.
19 Mark Rowlands, *The Philosopher and the Wolf: Lessons from the Wild on Love, Death, and Happiness*, Granta Books, London, 2008, p. 63.
20 Anthony Bourke & John Rendall, *A Lion Called Christian*, Broadway Books, New York, 1971, p. 38.
21 Jeffrey Masson & Susan McCarthy, *When Elephants Weep*, Vintage, London, 1996, p. 142.
22 Darwin, *Expression of the Emotions in Man and Animals*.
23 Charles Birch, *Feelings*, University of NSW Press, 1995.
24 United States Senate, *Report of the Senate Select Committee on Intelligence: Committee Study of the Central Intelligence Agency's Detention and Interrogation Program*, 2014, www.intelligence.senate.gov/sites/default/files/publications/CRPT-113srpt288.pdf; see also B. Carey, 'Architects of CIA interrogation drew on psychology to induce "helplessness"', *The New York Times*, 10 December 2014, www.nytimes.com/2014/12/11/health/architects-of-cia-interrogation-drew-on-psychology-to-induce-helplessness.html, and S. Shane, '2 US architects of harsh tactics in 9/11's wake', *The New York Times*, 11 August 2009, www.nytimes.com/2009/08/12/us/12psychs.html.
25 T. McCoy, '"Learned helplessness": the chilling psychological principle behind the CIA's interrogation methods', *The Washington Post*, 11 December 2014, www.washingtonpost.com/news/morning-mix/wp/2014/12/11/the-chilling-psychological-principle-behind-the-cias-interrogation-methods.
26 The Humane Society of the United States, 'Dogs used in experiments FAQ', no date, https://www.humanesociety.org/resources/dogs-used-experiments-faq#many.
27 Masson & McCarthy, *When Elephants Weep*.
28 Darwin, *Expression of the Emotions in Man and Animals*.
29 Bil Gilbert, *How Animals Communicate*, A&R, London, 1967.
30 C.S. Lewis, 'Vivisection', in *God in the Dock: Essays on Theology and Ethics*, ed. W. Hooper, Eerdmans, Grand Rapids, Michigan, 1970.
31 John King (ed.), *Commentaries on the First Book of Moses: Genesis Vol. 1*, Calvin Translation Society, Edinburgh, 1847.
32 T. Regan, 'Christianity and animal rights: the challenge and promise', *Religion Online*, 1990, www.religion-online.org/article/christianity-and-animal-rights-the-challenge-and-promise/.

33 Gilbert, *How Animals Communicate*, p. 169.
34 T. Regan, 'Philosopher Tom Regan on animal rights', *Famous Trials*, 1985, https://famous-trials.com/animalrights/2599-philosopher-tom-regan-on-animal-rights#:~:text=The%20fundamental%20wrong%20is%20the,predictable%20as%20it%20is%20regrettable.
35 *BBC News*, 'Confessions of a slaughterhouse worker', 6 January 2020, www.bbc.com/news/stories-50986683.
36 J. Slade & E. Alleyne, 'The psychological impact of slaughterhouse employment: a systematic literature review', *Trauma, Violence, & Abuse*, vol. 24, no. 2, 2021, https://doi.org/10.1177/15248380211030243; also see T. Khara, 'Animals suffer for meat production—and abattoir workers do too', *The Conversation*, 5 February 2020, https://theconversation.com/animals-suffer-for-meat-production-and-abattoir-workers-do-too-127506, and L. Chedekel, 'Psychological distress among slaughterhouse workers warrants further study', *Boston University*, 19 June 2017, https://www.bu.edu/sph/news/articles/2017/psychological-distress-among-slaughterhouse-workers-warrants-further-study/
37 Slade & Alleyne, op. cit.
38 ABC, *Four Corners: A Bloody Business*, 8 August 2011, https://www.abc.net.au/4corners/a-bloody-business---2011/2841918.
39 ABC, 'Mass slaughter and abuse of racehorses undermines industry's commitment to animal welfare', 17 October 2019, www.abc.net.au/news/2019-10-18/slaughter-abuse-of-racehorses-undermines-industry-animal-welfare/11603834.
40 Jonathan Safran Foer, *Eating Animals*, Bay Back Books, New York, 2009, p. 196.
41 Irene M. Pepperberg, *Alex & Me: How a Scientist and a Parrot Discovered a Hidden World of Animal Intelligence—and Formed a Deep Bond in the Process*, HarperCollins, New York, 2008, p .221.
42 ibid., p. 107.
43 M. Cartmill, 'Animal minds, animal dreams', *Natural History*, vol. 107, no. 2, 1998, pp. 16–20.
44 L. Sharpe, 'So you think you know why animals play...', *Scientific American*, 17 May 2011, https://blogs.scientificamerican.com/guest-blog/so-you-think-you-know-why-animals-play/.
45 P. McGreevy, J. Winther Christensen, U. König von Borstel & A. McLean, *Equitation Science*, John Wiley & Sons, New York, 2018, p. 20.
46 Gilbert, *How Animals Communicate*, p. 12.
47 M. Bekoff & J. Pierce, *Wild Justice: The Moral Lives of Animals*, University of Chicago Press, Chicago 2009, p. 80. Original emphasis.
48 ibid., p. 106.
49 ibid., p. 138.

50 Cecilia Heyes & Caroline Catmur, 'What happened to mirror neurons?', *Perspectives on Psychological Science*, vol. 17, no. 1, 2021, https://doi.org/10.1177/1745691621990638.
51 ibid., p. 17.
52 Bekoff & Pierce, *Wild Justice*, p. 79.
53 NPR, 'Do animals have morals?', 5 September 2014, www.npr.org/transcripts/338936897.
54 ABC Radio, 'Indigenous equine therapy in the Kimberley', 11 December 2021, www.abc.net.au/radionational/programs/saturdayextra/indigenous-equine-therapy-kimberley/13672034.
55 P. Crowley-Robinson, D.C. Fenwick & J.K. Blackshaw, 'A long-term study of elderly people in nursing homes with visiting and resident dogs', *Applied Animal Behaviour Science*, vol. 47, nos 1–2, 1996, pp. 137–148, https://doi.org/10.1016/0168-1591(95)01017-3.
56 M.R. Banks, L.M. Willoughby & W.A. Banks, 'Animal-assisted therapy and loneliness in nursing homes: use of robotic versus living dogs', *Journal of the American Medical Directors Association*, vol. 9, no. 3, 2008, pp.173–177, https://doi.org/10.1016/j.jamda.2007.11.007 and Saint Louis University, 'Doggie robot eases loneliness in nursing home residents as well as real dog, study finds', *Science Daily*, 26 February 2008, www.sciencedaily.com/releases/2008/02/080225213636.htm.
57 Huber Social, *'Pups in Prison' Social Impact Report: Serco, Southern Queensland Correctional Centre*, 2020, www.serco.com/media/5597/serco-pups-in-prison-social-impact-performance-report-2020-v3.pdf?1602549429.
58 H. Burke, 'Pets in prison: the rescue dogs teaching Californian inmates trust and responsibility', *The Guardian*, 19 April 2020, www.theguardian.com/lifeandstyle/2020/apr/19/pets-in-prison-the-rescue-dogs-teaching-californian-inmates-trust-and-responsibility.
59 Michael Pollan, *The Omnivore's Dilemma: A Natural History of Four Meals*, Penguin, New York, 2007, p. 4.
60 ibid., pp. 10–11.

Select Bibliography

Anonymous, *Domesticated Animals; Considered with reference to Civilization and the Arts*, John W. Parker, London, 1837.

Bekoff, Marc & Jessica Pierce, *Wild Justice: The Moral Lives of Animals*, University of Chicago Press, Chicago, 2009.

Birch, Charles, *Feelings*, University of NSW Press, Sydney, 1995.

Boone, J. Allen, *Kinship with All Life*, Harper & Row, New York, 1954.

Bourke, Anthony & John Rendall, *A Lion Called Christian*, Broadway Books, New York, 1971.

Evans, E.P., *The Criminal Prosecution and the Capital Punishment of Animals*, William Heinemann, London, 1906.

Darnton, Robert, *The Great Cat Massacre and Other Episodes in French Cultural History*, Basic Books, New York, 1984.

Darwin, Charles, *The Expression of the Emotions in Man and Animals*, John Murray, London, 1872.

Gilbert, Bil, *How Animals Communicate*, A&R, London, 1967.

Hempfling, Klaus Ferdinand, *Dancing with Horses*, Trafalgar Square Books, Vermont, 2001.

Hornung, Eva, *Dog Boy*, Text Publishing, Melbourne, 2010.

Griffin, Donald R., *Animal Minds: Beyond Cognition to Consciousness*, Chicago University Press, Chicago, 2001.

Griffin, Donald R., *Animal Thinking*, Harvard University Press, Cambridge, Mass, 1984.

King, John (ed.), *Commentaries on the First Book of Moses: Genesis Vol. 1*, Calvin Translation Society, Edinburgh, 1847.

McGreevy, P., J. Winther Christensen, U. König von Borstel & A. McLean, *Equitation Science*, John Wiley & Sons, New York 2018.

Masson, Jeffrey & Susan McCarthy, *When Elephants Weep: The Emotional Lives of Animals*, Vintage, London, 1996.

Pepperberg, Irene M., *Alex & Me: How a Scientist and a Parrot Discovered a Hidden World of Animal Intelligence—and Formed a Deep Bond in the Process*, HarperCollins, New York, 2008.

Pollan, Michael, *The Omnivore's Dilemma: A Natural History of Four Meals*, Penguin, New York, 2007.

Regan, Tom, *The Case for Animal Rights*, University of California Press, 1983.

Rowlands, Mark, *The Philosopher and the Wolf: Lessons from the Wild on Love, Death, and Happiness*, Granta Books, London, 2008.

Safran Foer, Jonathan, *Eating Animals*, Bay Back Books, New York, 2009.

Salatin, Joel, *Salad Bar Beef*, Polyface, USA, 1996.

Sheldrake, Rupert, *Dogs That Know When Their Owners Are Coming Home and Other Unexplained Powers of Animals*, Crown Publishing, New York, 2011.

Singer, Peter, *Animal Liberation*, Jonathan Cape, London, 1976.

Williams, Marta, *Beyond Words: Talking with Animals and Nature*, New World Library, Novato, California, 2005.

Williams, Marta, *Learning Their Language: Intuitive Communication with Animals and Nature*, New World Library, Novato, California, 2003.

Wise, Steven M., *Rattling the Cage: Towards Legal Rights for Animals*, Perseus Books, Cambridge, Massachusetts, 2000.

About Upswell

Upswell Publishing was established in 2021 by Terri-ann White as a not-for-profit press. A perceived gap in the market for distinctive literary works in fiction, poetry and narrative non-fiction was the motivation. In her years as a bookseller, writer and then publisher, Terri-ann has maintained a watch on literary books and the way they insinuate themselves into a cultural space and are then located within our literary and cultural inheritance. She is interested in making books to last: books with the potential to still be noticed, and noted, after decades and thus be ripe to influence new literary histories.

About this typeface

Book designer Becky Chilcott chose Foundry Origin not only as a strong, carefully considered, and dependable typeface, but also to honour her late friend and mentor, type designer Freda Sack, who oversaw the project. Designed by Freda's long-standing colleague, Stuart de Rozario, much like Upswell Publishing, Foundry Origin was created out of the desire to say something new.

www.ingramcontent.com/pod-product-compliance
Lightning Source LLC
Chambersburg PA
CBHW030647230426
43665CB00011B/986